More Praise for *Seeing Red C*

"Goodrich takes what could be c
style for action that works! I've se ... ...n. toolkit
takes the work out of the planning process and helps put it into
practice quickly. Her video *Seeing Red Cars* should be on the desk
of every leader, and this book should be on the desk and workstation
of all employees in your organization, especially in today's lean and
ever-demanding environment. Start seeing red cars to help keep your
organization a leader and out of the red."

—**Robert Scott, Retired Vice President and CSO, Advanced Bio-Medical
    Company**

"*Seeing Red Cars* by Laura Goodrich is not merely a metaphor. It is a
powerful catalyst for personal, team, and organizational transformation. In this important new book, Laura has masterfully captured the
critical element of success and failure: the focus of our attention.
Seeing Red Cars is a much-needed wake-up call, inviting readers
to shift their focus from what they don't want onto what they truly
want—and keep it there. Laura further provides a compelling formula
for action to bring one's focus from the domain of the imagination into
the arena of actualization. Having used her material with great success in my own leadership seminars, I can recommend *Seeing Red
Cars* without hesitation to anyone who wants to be more successful
in any area of life. Focus on the principles of *Seeing Red Cars* and
fasten your seat belt for an exciting ride to the future of your wants."

—**David Chard, former Director, Asia-Pacific Edelman Academy, and
    President, Engaging Minds, Hong Kong**

"*Seeing Red Cars* is one of the most powerful messages I have ever
come across. It's crazy good. It changed my thought process immediately. Goodrich offers a constant reminder to ask others and myself
what we want. I *thought* that I thought positively until I realized how
much room for improvement I have! It is not only the best personal
development process I've ever encountered, I believe that any organization can realize huge benefits from implementing this methodology.
I can't wait to share it with my customers and colleagues."

—**Kristin Ford, President, PC Training Source, and President, American
    Society for Training and Development, Twin Cities Chapter**

"*Seeing Red Cars* provides a fresh perspective on facilitating successful change and is a very useful extension to the material that Laura has previously covered in her film on the same topic. Goodrich includes great case studies based on real-world experience and combines this with easy-to-understand theory based on solid scientific research. *Seeing Red Cars* is a practical guide for managers and leaders seeking to lead change more effectively. It has a range of easy-to-use tools that can be leveraged by both individuals and teams seeking to adopt a more positive mind-set. The *Seeing Red Cars* concept is also fun, which is an important element in getting people to buy into a new approach."

—**Tony Ritchie, Vice President for Technology, Asia Pacific Region, for a Fortune 100 company**

"Goodrich has made it easy to focus on 'what I do like' about her book. Any book that identifies how a single change in mind-set can make a profound, positive difference in our lives is a book worth reading. The concept of *Seeing Red Cars* is elegance on wheels."

—**Leo Bottary, Vice President, Public Affairs, Vistage International, and Adjunct Professor, Master of Arts in Strategic Communication and Leadership program, Seton Hall University**

"*Seeing Red Cars* is a must-read for anyone who is interested in individual or organizational transformation. As a human resources executive and life coach, I strongly recommend the book. The scientific knowledge is presented in an easy-to-read and engaging manner. The practical tools walk you through a process all readers can follow to bring about change in their company or their own life."

—**Lesa Hammond, PhD, Assistant Vice President for Human Resources, Mills College**

SEEING RED CARS

SEEING RED CARS

Driving yourself, your team,
and your organization
to a positive future

Laura Goodrich

BK®

Berrett–Koehler Publishers, Inc.
San Francisco
a BK Life book

Berrett-Koehler Publishers, Inc.
235 Montgomery Street, Suite 650
San Francisco, CA 94104-2916
Tel: (415) 288-0260   Fax: (415) 362-2512   www.bkconnection.com

Ordering Information

Quantity sales. Special discounts are available on quantity purchases by corporations, associations, and others. For details, contact the "Special Sales Department" at the Berrett-Koehler address above.

Individual sales. Berrett-Koehler publications are available through most bookstores. They can also be ordered directly from Berrett-Koehler: Tel: (800) 929-2929; Fax: (802) 864-7626; www.bkconnection.com

Orders for college textbook/course adoption use. Please contact Berrett-Koehler: Tel: (800) 929-2929; Fax: (802) 864-7626.

Orders by U.S. trade bookstores and wholesalers. Please contact Ingram Publisher Services, Tel: (800) 509-4887; Fax: (800) 838-1149; E-mail: customer.service@ingrampublisherservices.com; or visit www.ingrampublisherservices.com/Ordering for details about electronic ordering.

Berrett-Koehler and the BK logo are registered trademarks of Berrett-Koehler Publishers, Inc.

Printed in the United States of America

Berrett-Koehler books are printed on long-lasting acid-free paper. When it is available, we choose paper that has been manufactured by environmentally responsible processes. These may include using trees grown in sustainable forests, incorporating recycled paper, minimizing chlorine in bleaching, or recycling the energy produced at the paper mill.

Library of Congress Cataloging-in-Publication Data
Goodrich, Laura.
    Seeing red cars : think it, see it, do it! : driving yourself, your team, and your organization to a positive future / Laura Goodrich. — 1st ed.
        p. cm.
Includes bibliographical references and index.
ISBN 978-1-60509-727-5 (pbk. original : alk. paper)
    1. Organizational change. 2. Organizational behavior. 3. Organizational effectiveness. I. Title.
HD58.8.G665 2011
658.4'063--dc22   2010044053

First Edition

15 14 13 12 11 10   9 8 7 6 5 4 3 2 1

Cover design: Pemastudio
Text design and paging: Adriane Bosworth
Illustrator: Camilla Coates
Proofreader: Susan Padgett
Indexer: Kirsten Kite

This book is dedicated to my husband, RICK, *the most supportive and honorable man I have ever known, and to my amazing kids,* MADI *and* JUDD, *who inspire me every day.*

Contents

Preface

A Note to Plan Ahead: If you plan to read this book while traveling, please *download the Seeing Red Cars Toolkit PDF before you leave* from www.seeingredcarsbook.com so you'll be prepared to complete the Red Cars exercises as you go.

Seeing Red Cars is a metaphor for focusing on what you want. It acts as a visual trigger to remind you of the positive outcomes you are striving for and, when you stray off the track, to jog your memory back into the present and refocus on what you want personally and professionally. This book is based on more than 15 years of lessons learned from working with people, teams, and organizations that struggled as they were living and working in times of dynamic change. To help these and other companies better deal with the challenges, my partner Greg Stiever and I produced the powerful film *Seeing Red Cars* that already, at the time I am writing, is being used by more than 500 trainers, coaches, and consultants worldwide as part of their existing training curriculums or to establish employees' positive focus and engagement when they are launching important change initiatives. This book digs deeper into the *Seeing Red Cars* positive outcomes mind-set and guides you in making intentional changes that will have an impact on your life.

Breaking the Pattern of Focusing on "I Don't Wants"

My name is Laura Goodrich, and I love working with individuals, teams, and organizations to create cultures grounded in effective workplace dynamics. Many of the companies I have worked with were undergoing significant change, and I loved helping people get past the reactionary phase and ultimately begin seeing themselves as part of the solution. I loved helping employees craft the go-forward direction and establish the strategy to support it.

Through these experiences and through the process of training and coaching hundreds of executives and other people around the world, I witnessed a phenomenon that played itself out repeatedly: People's natural inclination is to focus on what they do *not* want to have happen, not on what they *do* want to have happen. It happened so often that I started recognizing the pattern. When I asked people what they want, without hesitation they would say, "What I don't want is this: I don't want people to be gone that day, I don't want to be stood up at meetings, I don't want to waste my time." Even after I repeatedly pointed out that their statements began with "I don't want" and I specifically asked them to rephrase their statements as "I wants," they quickly returned to expressing what they didn't want or what they were trying to avoid.

When people intentionally change their focus to what they *do* want, phenomenal events start happening in their business and personal lives. And when a group of employees or an entire team or organization gets on board and focuses on what they *do* want, positive outcomes replicate, and achieving corporate objectives becomes even more possible.

What puzzled me for some time was how to cause that shift from focusing on what you don't want and are trying to avoid to a positive mind-set. I longed to help people understand how to:

1. Resist the natural inclination to focus on negative thoughts, concerns, and fears.

2. Create a sense of awareness around their individual interests, passions, strengths, and values.

3. Make the connection between their personal and professional "I wants" and those of their team and organization to create individual and collective positive outcomes.

I had seen what can happen when people choose to concentrate on positive outcomes and ultimately succeed in influencing the collective goals and objectives of teams and organizations.

While I was pondering this question, my business partner, Greg Stiever, was telling wonderful and emotional stories through his video camera. When we met, Greg had 25 years of experience as a digital storyteller and Emmy Award–winning producer. I had spent my life in front of the camera, and Greg was the pro behind the camera. When we began collaborating in 2007 and formed On Impact, we discovered how to blend our talents in a powerful way by using digital storytelling to help companies and organizations influence positive change. The first result of our collaboration is the *Seeing Red Cars* metaphor with support materials, a film, and now a book with a toolkit of activities that turn insight into action and action into outcomes. We are excited to offer this book to help individuals, teams, and organizations grasp these concepts and put them to work toward their own personal and professional successes.

The tremendous response to the *Seeing Red Cars* film was the impetus for writing this book. On www.seeingredcarsbook.com are the Red Cars Toolkit and a variety of additional supplemental Red Cars items and activities to build individual understanding and clarity and to engage people at all levels. They can be used to develop a long-term program to drive your organization's positive change. They contribute to the effort to extend the experience and keep Red Cars in focus for meaningful change to occur.

Who *Seeing Red Cars* Is For

Individuals, teams, and organizations seeking to improve their personal and professional lives and to take actions to put their passions, interests, strengths, and values to work will benefit from reading this book. We'll describe step-by-step how people can pinpoint their greatest strengths and values and align them with the right organizational vision, mission, and values. Sometimes that will be with their current employer, and sometimes not. The most important factor is to be courageous enough to ask the right questions, talk to the right people, and figure out for yourself what environment is best for you.

Many have advanced the cause of focusing on your goals. *Seeing Red Cars* takes this cause from the personal perspective, "It starts with you," and makes frequent and meaningful tie-ins to corporate America through the wonderful use of stories—real-life stories (some with made-up names to protect the identities of former clients) that help you visualize and internalize the messages and meanings. Many of the stories are also available as short videos and audios on www.seeingredcarsbook.com so you can incorporate them into your company's programs.

Where the Journey Will Take You

We start by introducing the concept of focusing on what you want and the difference it can make when you choose this positive outcomes mind-set. Chapter 1, "Why We Focus on What We Don't Want," discusses how the brain works and why this unconscious natural tendency is so ghastly hard to change. Chapter 2, "Rewire Your Brain for Better Outcomes," introduces strategies you can use to literally rewire your brain and create better outcomes. "Play to Your Strengths and Control What You Can," Chapter 3, helps you identify your top passions or interests and personal strengths and stresses the importance of focusing on what you *can* control. Chapter 4, "Tune in and Take Charge," addresses how to be keenly aware of and curious about marketplace dynamics and trends so you can steer your thoughts, actions, and learning. In "Craft Personal 'I Wants'" and "Craft Professional 'I Wants,'" Chapters 5 and 6, you'll roll up your sleeves and complete the Red Cars Toolkit to clarify your personal and professional "I wants." In Chapter 7, "Turn Actions into Outcomes," you'll create an action traction plan to record and track action steps so you will *stick with it* for the long haul. The final chapter, "Drive Red Cars to Critical Mass," tells the culminating story of an organization that built a culture of people focused on their wants and the marked difference it has made to the company's success.

How to Use This Book

Follow the process described in this book if you truly want to build a positive future for yourself and a *Seeing Red Cars* culture in your team and organization. If your company is reeling from the economic downturn and you want to forge a path back to prosperity, you as an individual, your team, and your organization must embrace a positive outcomes mind-set. *Seeing Red Cars* is a powerful metaphor with supporting materials, videos, and activities around which you can build impactful and sustaining change. Start by reading the book yourself, completing the Red Cars activities, and plotting your own course. Then spread the word to others and encourage them to do the same. Thoughtful planning and actions toward your individual and collective "I wants" and driving with intention and your high beams on will position you, your team, and your organization for achieving success.

A note to leaders: This book offers a powerful toolkit and methodology to influence positive outcomes in your organization. Change is the new norm, and innovations are accelerating. The companies that ultimately survive and thrive will enable their employees to focus on their passions, interests, strengths, and values and to align these with the vision and values of the company. The *Seeing Red Cars* mind-set can guide employees in the development of personal and professional "I wants" that are recorded as monthly, weekly, and daily actions. When an entire organization of individuals is *Seeing Red Cars* and finally hits critical mass with this positive outcomes mind-set, great things happen.

Prepare for an awesome trip.

Focus on What You Want

You could be getting more of what you want—more new ideas, more teamwork in your department, and a more positive attitude in the company. I believe that people want to succeed in their jobs, in their relationships, and throughout their communities. I believe that people want to build the lives they want and be a part of something productive and positive. Too often, it doesn't work out that way.

Through my experiences in workplace dynamics, change, and the future, I have learned one overriding truth: You get more of whatever you focus on. Let me repeat: You get more of *whatever* you focus on. I call it *Seeing Red Cars* because the metaphor is one that everyone can relate to. Here is the premise:

Say you recently bought your dream car—custom wheels, full chrome bumpers, and it's red. Driving it home for the first time, you start noticing something. It seems like there are a lot of red cars out there. The next day, what do you notice? There are *definitely* more red cars on the road. By the end of the first week, you're thinking, "Is everyone driving a red car?" You're seeing red cars because that's what you're focused on.

Or how about this: It's every golfer's nightmare. You're standing at the signature hole, elevated T to a large green, a short par 3, only 130 yards over water—*lots* of water. You take out your pitching wedge and stare at the water. You take a last look at your ball and you're thinking, "Don't hit it in the water. Don't hit it in the water!" Finally, you hit the ball. Where does it go? *Splat*—straight into the water.

One more example to make the point: One of your coworkers is really getting on your nerves. To make matters worse, you keep running into this person in every meeting, in the hallway, at lunch, in the parking lot. You can't escape.

Who's putting all these thoughts of "red cars," "don't hit it in the water," and "I can't get away from this person" into your head? You are, of course. It's what you're focused on. And remember what I said: Whether good or bad, you *always* get more of what you focus on.

Even when someone's intentions are genuinely positive, their actual behaviors can come across as negative without their knowledge. Here is an example:

Several years ago, I received a call from a client in desperate need of answers (we'll call him Ted). Ted was managing a high-profile project. The stakes were high, and the project was off track; timelines were slipping, budgets were busting, and the dynamics of the group were strained. He proceeded to describe his observations. Team members were avoiding him at all costs. In meetings, tensions were so high that he didn't know what was worse: the angry outbursts or the deafening silence that followed. People were blaming others, and without conscious intention, they were coming to meetings late or not at all. Ted was chasing the excuses without success and was at his wit's end. We decided I would shadow him to see if we could flush out the culprit for the unproductive behaviors.

I followed Ted for a day. I stood next to him through his team one-to-ones and meetings large and small. It didn't take long to see what was going on. I watched him begin each conversation and meeting with statements like these: "You know, we don't want to miss this timeline, we don't want to seem uncooperative, we don't want to go over budget, we don't want to fail." When I share this story, people always ask, "Was he clueless? What was wrong with him?" To this I say, "There was nothing wrong with him. He was doing something that was unconscious. He had the best intentions for the team and the project. He had seen projects fail and was committed to avoiding the pitfalls. He had a laundry list of things he did not want to have happen, and he was quick to make others aware of them. He thought he was being helpful."

In actuality, his team worked hard. As a result, they had missed family gatherings and their kids' games and had taken little time to rest and rejuvenate. When Ted began each interaction with a reminder of what he did not want to happen, he inadvertently sucked the energy, motivation, and spirit out of each person.

I talked to Ted about the *Seeing Red Cars* mind-set: Focus on what you *do* want to happen. Once he became aware, he suddenly got it. He met with each team member to share his learning. The discussion was telling, as they described how his focus had made them feel frustrated, unappreciated, and unmotivated.

Together, Ted and his team members wrote personal and project "I want" statements (an intentional action step from *Seeing Red Cars*). He coached the team to share their "I want" statements, the status of each, and their strategy for moving the project along in one-to-one and project meetings. Team members were asked to align their professional "I want" statements with those of the project, and before long, they were back on track, working collaboratively, and producing the daily, weekly, and monthly actions needed to succeed.

As they adopted a positive-outcomes mind-set at both the individual and team levels, it eventually spread to other areas of the company and affected the division's overall performance.

You Must Consciously Break the Pattern

Focusing on what we don't want has a reach far greater than we realize. It is our natural tendency, and it's been going on a long time.

Do you remember third-grade reading class? Most people I talk to remember the same thing. You're sitting with your group at the reading table, and everyone has to take turns reading. Pretty soon it's your turn. Chances are, while your classmates were reading, you weren't even listening. You were mentally counting how many more students before it's your turn. Your fear builds, your heart pounds, your hands tremble, and you can't stop thinking how hard it is. Finally, it's your turn. One agonizing word at a time, you finally get through the paragraph. And you make it through the day, and you make it through third grade. And it doesn't ever really go away.

Now you've moved from the classroom to the conference room. They're not your classmates, they're your colleagues. You're all supposed to give your reports. And you're doing it again—wondering which direction they're going to go around the table. You're still focused on not wanting to make a mistake, on not wanting to look foolish, and your heart pounds. Why does this happen? Why do we spend time and energy dealing with fear and obstacles instead of taking action to move in the right direction? It's so simple we can recognize it in others, and yet it's so subtle we don't see it in ourselves. That's the problem. We don't realize that we're focused on what we don't want.

Raising your consciousness will help you begin moving in the opposite direction. One small shift makes a big difference. It may sound easy, but it's not. The hard work is focusing on what you want to happen and not on what you are trying to avoid.

Think It

Similar to the Law of Attraction, start by making a commitment to focus your thoughts on what you want, not on what you don't want. Write down specifically what you want. Make a contract with yourself.

See It

Now picture it in your mind. The more vividly you can picture the desired outcome, with every detail, the better. Many people find and display pictures that illustrate their desires. They find it very motivational and effective.

Identify pictures that depict what you want. I'm not talking about material things. I'm referring to things like successful projects, growth and professional development, new skills, and an amazing family unit. What do these look like to you?

Focus on the goal. More important than the words you say to others are the words you say to yourself.

Do It

Put these intentions into action. Become aware of what you're focusing on, and focus on what you can control instead of on what you can't. Practice and be persistent.

I am a host on a Twin Cities television show called *Life to the Max*, produced by the Lifetouch Corporation (the K–12 school portrait photography and yearbook company). On the show, I tell the stories of people with special talents, people who persevere when it would be easier to quit, and people who have the self-discipline to put in the time. Renowned painter Jeffrey Hurinenko is one of those people.

In the interview, I asked Jeff what it takes to be as good as he is. He said, "You can have all the talent in the world. You can study art all day long. But if you want to get *really* good, you've got to be willing to put in the miles." He calls it "brush mileage." You have to close yourself off from others and put in the time with a brush and canvas.

In Malcolm Gladwell's book *Outliers*, the author discusses the fact that people who have achieved greatness—whether in sports, music, or business—have clocked 10,000 hours of brush mileage or sweat equity to achieve success. Be persistent and practice.

Celebrate Success

All the while you are focusing on what you want and taking actions toward your goals, celebrate your successes. For many of us, our projects are long. Celebrating when they are completed could literally mean years. A sales executive once wrote me a note that it was this teaching point he most appreciated, and he is now a lot better at practicing it. His sales process is drawn out and requires input from multiple entities within his organization. He said that breaking the long, drawn-out process into milestones and celebrating along the way really keeps him going.

It Takes Awareness

It is very easy to slip back into focusing on what you don't want. To turn things around, you have to catch yourself when your thoughts, actions, and words don't line up. To illustrate:

> *No one would say:* "What I want is to engage in a conversation and say something offensive so that the other person says something that is equally or even more offensive. I'll then respond in kind and storm away from the conversation steaming mad."

We would never say that, and yet it happens.

Let's say the same person has created an "I want" statement with a mental and emotional image to support that statement.

> *The "I want" statement is:* "I want to effectively manage conversations so that I bring out the best in others and create trusted and open communication."

This person has thought of a mental image of herself and what she is thinking and feeling when she is engaged in an effective conversation, and she can recall the image, her inner feelings, and the associated thought process at any time. When she is in a conversation and happens to say something the other person perceives as offensive, she immediately recalls this image. Suddenly, she responds in a creative way that brings out the best in the other person and creates trusted and open communication. Without the guide of the "I want" statement and its mental and emotional image, these moments all too often head south.

I have had so many clients report a dramatic improvement in conversations and relationships, both personally and professionally, with "I want" statements and visualization of what they want. Additionally, once you see it clearly in your mind, you'll naturally begin taking action toward what you want.

How Does This Apply to the Business World?

Companies can control the mind-set from which problems, challenges, and opportunities are communicated to the workforce. Here is an example of what often happens when a major change is occurring in an organization.

Acme Manufacturing has been slowly trending downward. Orders have been falling over the past few quarters. Mike, its chief financial officer, alerts CEO Jerry of the problem. It's not Mike's fault, of course, but the indicators of problems were more obvious from his vantage point. Jerry convenes an emergency meeting with his key leadership in which the need for change is made clear. After the news is out on the table, there is a period of time when the leaders simply try to get their bearings. After pulling themselves together, they begin to consider possible solutions. Once they identify the best course of action, they establish a strategy to support it. After much debate and planning, the day comes to reveal the circumstances and proposed change to the masses.

At that point, Jerry and his executive staff have been discussing the process for months. They have had plenty of time to think through the nuances and ramifications of the change, particularly as it relates to their own roles and responsibilities.

Jerry makes a big company-wide presentation with the hopes that everyone will see the light, they'll grab hold of the new direction, and life will be sweet. People listen as long as they hear something that has the potential to really have an impact on their world. As soon as something is said that has direct personal implications, they redirect their attention inward and begin focusing on it. More specifically, they focus on what they fear and what they hope to avoid through the process. They don't hear anything else Jerry says.

Jerry completes his presentation and steps down from the stage with high hopes. Instead, he is bombarded with expressions that show fear and questions. The resistance is obvious, and both sides of the equation are confused and, frankly, kind of mad. Jerry and his executive staff think, "Hey, everything we are proposing is for the greater good. Can't you see this?" Truth be told, they can't, not yet, and for some, not ever.

Jerry and his senior leaders let the moment pass with the hope that things will improve with time. Instead, they get worse. People begin talking and hashing out the details. Questions come up and are answered with assumptions rather than facts. The plot thickens. The leaders close their doors because the conversations aren't fun and they quickly tire of the repetitive nature of the questions. They think, "My gosh, how many times have I heard this question? I already addressed this in the big presentation, but they weren't listening." As I said, they had retreated inside their own heads to consider the ramifications of item 1 on a list of 20. So the leaders are left to deal with the aftershock. They have their own concerns and would love to offer their honest two cents, but they gut it out for the sake of the organization.

Conversely, this is a real-life example of how a division leader used *Seeing Red Cars* prior to announcing a branch closing and was thanked for the humane way in which she delivered the bad news.

Carol is a division vice president for National Widget Corporation. The depressed economic environment forced Carol to make the difficult decision to close an entire branch of the business. A meeting of all employees was convened. Carol began by showing the *Seeing Red Cars* film. When the lights were turned back on, she spoke candidly about her disappointment in having to make the decision and how she knew it was disappointing for everyone. Then she asked for their help. Carol told attendees to break into small groups, each with a leader, and record the "I wants" of their group in light of this change.

When the participants had arrived, they had such thoughts as "I don't want to lose my job" foremost in their minds. Once they were given the opportunity to have honest dialogue and discuss their feelings in a productive way, statements like this emerged: "I want to develop an opportunity for myself either here or elsewhere that makes use of my skills and talents" and "We want to contribute to realigning people and resources when this division closes to make the company even stronger."

The "I wants" set the tone toward a positive outlook, and a very productive session followed. Once people realized they could contribute their ideas and their thoughts were being heard, they relaxed. Their body language visibly changed. It proved to be a very powerful format with a positive outcome.

In the days following the meeting, Carol received an outpouring of e-mail thanking her for her leadership through the difficulty of closing the branch. *Seeing Red Cars* united management and employees and led them to proactive decision-making in a time of crisis.

The need for change Acme Manufacturing and National Widget Corporation faced is now the current dynamic in which we all live. Rapid marketplace changes can quickly affect the demand for your organization's products and services. The realization that an organization needs to change may come from financial folks, as in the Acme Manufacturing example, or from sources such as exit interviews, employee climate surveys, or customer feedback. It may come from new innovations that create new opportunities. Regardless of the source, it is important to not ignore the signals.

The economic downturn has changed the business landscape, and many say it will never be the same again. Most organizations will be forced to change. All of this uncertainty simply exacerbates our natural tendency to focus on what we don't want. It is critically important for individuals, teams, and organizations to maintain focus on what they want, especially in light of unforeseen changes. Those who are able to respond to change creatively and innovatively will have the clear advantage over those who react to change with avoidance and fear.

Now is the time to rock up onto our toes, clearly define what we want, and take definitive actions toward it. There is no time like the present. The reality is that one thing leads to another, whether it is positive *or* negative. It takes conscious effort and persistence to make sure that the thoughts and behaviors being spread are positive. Small successes and large achievements all start in the same way. Somebody focuses on what they want, and by doing so, they begin the journey of making it happen.

It isn't easy. In my work with clients over the years, I found myself scratching my head countless times when the need for change had been clearly identified. The team realized that if it remained on its current course, the end destination would not be one that anyone would choose, given an option. With this reality, a new direction was introduced. In many cases, there was no other viable option. I would think, "Why would you object to the only hope of survival or a positive outcome?" The direction that was being recommended may have been right or it may have been wrong, but it was clearly better than ignoring the signals that the team was in serious trouble, right? People still dug in their heels. Curious, I thought.

Core to the *Seeing Red Cars* positive outcome mind-set is an unwavering focus despite obstacles and criticism. This mind-set must begin with you and then spread to your team and organization. The following story from the *Seeing Red Cars* film is a wonderful example of the tremendous potential of a singular, unwavering focus on a goal. Imagine what could be accomplished with a whole work team of Cliff Youngs.

In 1983, Cliff Young decided to run the Sydney-to-Melbourne Ultra Marathon Race. The six-day, 875-kilometer run is considered to be the world's toughest race. That's more than 500 miles! Only the most elite runners are up to the challenge.

Ready to go, Young, a 61-year-old farmer, is wearing a sweater and galoshes. When the marathon starts, the runners leave Young and his galoshes behind. The crowds laugh because he appears to be shuffling his feet instead of running correctly. Mockingly, it is called the "Young Shuffle." But because he never read a book on racing and never talked to another runner, at night, when everyone else is sleeping, he shuffles right by them, nonstop for five and a half days. Young won that race. He broke the record by nine hours. He knew what he wanted, focused on that, and kept running.

When people try new approaches, they are often mocked until the new approaches are proven to work. They need to have the courage to press on and not be deterred by others' comments or snickers. Since Cliff Young's success, the Young shuffle has been adopted by other ultramarathon runners because it expends less energy. Young's story is one of dedication and determination and a clear example of achieving success through focusing on what you want.

You know what your options are: more of what you don't want or more of what you want. It's time to make the right choice. Focus on what you really do want. It's waiting out there for you.

CHAPTER 1

Why We Focus on What We Don't Want

*W*hen I introduce the concept of *Seeing Red Cars*, people immediately understand it from two perspectives.

1. They understand that it's really important to focus on what we want because the more we focus on and take action toward what we want, the more we're going to get back. They understand that intuitively. They understand that logically.

2. When it's brought to their attention, they also understand the natural inclination to focus on what we don't want. I can explain this concept to an 8-year-old or an 80-year-old, and everyone understands it. They recognize that if you're going to play a game, you're going to focus on winning that game. They recognize that race car drivers focus on the track, not on the walls they're trying to avoid.

There are two predominant reasons why it is so ghastly hard to change behaviors:

1. It is estimated that we have 12,000 to 50,000 thoughts coursing through our brains each day, and 70% of them are focused on what we don't want and what we'd like to avoid.

2. When people encounter important new information, there are three typical reactions: 20% are very open and excited

about it, 50% are cautious and not forthcoming with their support, and 30% are openly opposed.

Insights from Brain Research

As I've been working with corporations on workforce behaviors and dealing with change, my desire grew to understand why we focus on what we don't want. I am a thought leader in workplace dynamics, change, and the future of work. I am not a neuroscientist. Therefore, I sought answers from the scientific community.

Over the years, I have been fortunate to collaborate with a number of people who have dedicated their careers to brain research. I'll share enough about what I've learned about the brain to provide understanding and awareness, without causing overload, because the brain is a very, very complex entity. We still have so much to learn about the quadrillions of synapses that occur in the brain. (A synapse is a gap between two nerve cells. Neurons are cells that pass signals to individual target cells, and synapses are the means by which they do so.)

Ellen Weber is CEO of the MITA Brain Institute. Brain research is her business. Specifically, she translates brain research into human behavior, in particular, human behavior within organizations. When I asked Dr. Weber what causes us to focus on what we don't want, she explained that it is a combination of social conditioning and life experiences. We develop a fear-based response that begins with our unique genes and is socially conditioned within our families. Well-intentioned parents say things to their kids like "Don't run!" "Don't get hurt!" and "Don't act out!" Their good intentions are to protect their children, but in reality, they create a fear-based reaction. Sometimes it's real; sometimes it's perceived. For instance, you might come from a family that has a tendency to worry or that has a kind of victim mentality (always thinking someone is "after them").

Our genetic makeup partially determines our reactions, and families are the first place that social conditioning begins. Influence continues with our schools and includes the people we hang around with, the work we do, and the environment with which we surround ourselves. In a recent presentation, I discussed social conditioning and family influence. Afterward, a mother told me, "You spoke to me today. Before I left home this morning I said to my son David, 'Don't act out. Don't overreact.' Now that you bring this up, it makes perfect sense that I should give him direction he can actually act on in a positive way. It would have been better to say, 'Have good listening ears today and remember to pay attention to your teacher's directions. Try standing by Joey. He makes good decisions.'" I told her that she's right and can take it one step further by coaching David to focus on what he wants. She could say, "David, how would you like gym class to go today? What will you need to do for that to happen?" She can ask David questions that prompt him to think of specific things he can do. "Which classmates are doing well in the class and could help you do these things?" I told her she might think that David is too young to respond positively to coaching like this, but no matter what their age, kids are capable of focusing on what they want, and the sooner you help them pave pathways toward what they want, the better. This is perhaps the most compelling reason to adopt the *Seeing Red Cars* mind-set and teach it to your kids. It's one of the best ways to help our children accomplish what they want.

Early social conditioning is what starts to create a sense of fear or concern with things like the unknown, failure, loss of social stature, and new and different things. Coaching children early on, like the example of David, steers social conditioning toward positive rather than negative outcomes.

Another reason we focus on what we don't want is that we do not think we are capable or deserving. Again, this comes from social conditioning. If you come from a background of humble means, you and your family members may think, "People like us don't get a PhD." This can be a powerful mental block that prevents you from even trying. Robert Fritz, an expert in developing creative capacities, says that two common beliefs get in the way of accomplishing what we want. Number one is the common belief in our powerlessness, our inability to bring into being all the things we really care about. Number two is unworthiness, that we do not deserve to have what we truly desire. Self-talk like this causes inaction and reverting to autopilot. The key to overcoming this threat is awareness. With self-realization that negative social conditioning can get in the way, you can turn on your relentless intention to root out the ways your thoughts are limiting or deceiving you. Challenge those thoughts and forge new pathways of thinking and taking actions toward your wants.

In *The Fifth Discipline*, Peter Senge discusses the powerful tension between where you are now and what you want by using an illustration with rubber bands to symbolize the tension. Picture yourself in the middle, facing right. Behind you, on the left, is a pole, and in front of you, on the right, is a large hand. You're in the middle with two rubber bands around your waist—one rubber band stretched around your waist and the pole on the left and the other rubber band stretched around your waist and the hand on the right. Both rubber bands are taut.

Opposite forces exist at all times when you are not content with the way things are today and you have specific "I wants" you are striving for. These forces act like rubber bands pulling you in opposite directions. The key is to acknowledge these forces and to plan and take purposeful actions so that you remain in control. Inaction pulls you toward the "I don't want" mind-set, on the left side, while intentional actions pull you toward the positive outcomes you want, on the right.

Another factor is real-life experiences. For instance, if you've had a car accident, it is only natural to focus on what you don't want: another car accident. This is especially true if you have a natural proclivity toward introspection. Years ago, my friend accidentally fell into the music pit at a concert and broke her leg. It's only natural that she does not want to fall into a music pit again. Even though the possibility of this ever happening again is remote, her eyes are wide open to situations in which she could reinjure herself.

Fear and Concern Trigger Negative Emotional Reactions

The brain plays a major role in the tendency to focus on what we don't want. In our brains, the amygdala controls the automatic responses associated with fear and concern. Think of it as the brain's place to store all our reactions to good and bad situations over a lifetime. It's the seat of our emotional responses. When we encounter something that we're afraid of or concerned about, the amygdala is good. As Dr. Weber says, "Panic reactions stored in the amygdala can cause us to get off the road when a Mack truck is barreling around the corner." That is good. That is helpful. Without the amygdala's familiar and learned reactions, we might show up to a meeting without clothes, if at all. This, too, is helpful. The trouble is that, due to our genetics, social conditioning, and life experiences, the amygdala has a difficult time distinguishing the difference between the threat of being hit by a Mack truck, the anxiety of asking for a raise, and the emotion of a challenging conversation. You may not be paralyzed with fear, but the brain is reacting very similarly. Whenever the amygdala reacts with fear or anxiety, it causes the release of harmful chemicals such as cortisol. The chemical reaction from cortisol has some limited redeeming qualities, but the first and last items on the list are certainly not desirable: high blood pressure and belly fat. If those reasons aren't enough to avoid it, here are some others: inability to focus, lack of creativity, and lack of innovation and resourcefulness. Fortunately, we can detour around the amygdala's negative reactions by storing reactions that lead us to more delightful goals, so that our brain doesn't land in the "I'm freaked" zone.

The amygdala creates a damaging pattern of reactions, which we can avoid. We can guide the amygdala to work in our favor by storing responses we'd like others to see in us—and we in ourselves—so that these responses emerge when we need them most. It is not easy, given our social conditioning and life experiences, but with the right intention and discipline, we can react well to tough situations and thereby alter our brain's chemical and electrical circuitry to move us toward what we want in any given situation. This is important: Take it one small step at a time. When you attempt too big a change, you trigger fear and avoidance. Take small, steady, incremental steps.

Creating New Roads Triggers Positive Responses

Instead of cortisol, you can choose to rewrite the typical responses stored in the amygdala to produce an opposite chemical reaction and release serotonin, which lends itself to creativity, innovation, and focus. It's why some people are just a lot more fun to be around. These are the people others like to work with and who are often asked to be part of projects. They have a natural tendency to come up with important solutions and responses to challenges.

Many wonderful benefits await people who act on what recent research suggests: Axons and dendrites can regenerate, regardless of your age, through the process of neuroplasticity, which means fresh rewiring. It is the secret to change and the answer to how we can reroute our brain's natural inclination to focus on what we don't want. We can grow, regenerate, and pave new neuron pathways toward our goals.

Neuroplasticity is defined as the brain's natural ability to form new connections to compensate for injury or environmental changes. A neuron is a nerve cell. Our brains have 100 billion of them, and you can march yours in your favor with carefully crafted activity. Neurons have extensions that are called dendrite brain cells. These extensions connect and reconnect. Axons, in contrast, relay information from the body back to the brain. In a complex electrochemical process, neurons communicate with each other in synapse, and the connection creates chemicals called neural transmitters. Each synapse begins creating a neural pathway.

The brain cells you obliterated in college or at the New Year's bash are gone for good, but luckily our brains can rebuild cells, strengthen remaining cells, and build new connections that compensate for those lost each day. Brains use the outside world to shape and reshape themselves physically and mentally. This means we can alter bad habits and add new approaches, such as focusing on what we want and aligning our thoughts, actions, and behaviors toward desired outcomes. It's like building a new road for your neurons and then acting on the desired changes. Your brain restructures to facilitate the process.

The reason it is hard to form those new pathways is that we have those estimated 12,000 to 50,000 thoughts coursing through our brains each day, and 70% of them are focused on what we don't want and what we'd like to avoid. Since a large percentage of our thoughts, actions, and behaviors are repetitive, inadvertently we create deep neural ruts that are hard to get out of and hard to change. It reminds me of driving on long stretches of freeway in South Dakota in the winter. The accumulation of ice on the well-traveled roadways creates deep ruts. It's much easier to let the tires roll in those ruts than to try to get out of them.

Awareness, Expectation, and Intention Drive Positive Outcomes

When you're consciously aware and you act on what you want to have happen, your brain responds by creating a road in. Change comes to the human brain with intention and consciously repetitive, step-by-step action toward future change. Whichever direction our prominent thoughts lean—either positively or negatively—our brains produce chemical reactions that attract more of those outcomes. The following story illustrates this reality.

I put myself through college working in a medical clinic. Carol and Rebecca worked at the front desk. They were similar in many ways: cheerful, helpful, and committed to doing the job well. As similar as they were, their daily experiences could not have been more different.

Rebecca seemed to attract the disgruntled patient. Scarcely a day went by when she didn't get berated and publicly challenged by a frustrated patient. Carol, on the other hand, rarely had such an encounter. When she did, she was able to turn the tide quickly. I often imagined their dinner conversations—Rebecca lamenting the crabby, mean-spirited patients and stressful work environment, and Carol commenting about the current trends of the flu.

What differentiated their experiences? Largely, expectation, a state of mind! Carol expected a fluid day at the clinic, and it often was. Before things got off track, Carol's expectations for the day would propel her into action. She'd quickly smooth slightly ruffled feathers before things got totally disheveled. She'd extend a confident smile and self-assured demeanor that left people feeling secure that they were in good hands.

Rebecca, on the other hand, focused on what she didn't want and got more of it. She didn't want to be yelled at, and she got yelled at. She didn't want charts to get misplaced, and they often did, especially charts of regular patients we knew had short fuses. Rebecca was focused on what she didn't want. For that reason, anticipating situations before they happened wasn't even on Rebecca's radar. She reacted in the moment; she reacted with fear. Often you could see her posture anticipating the blow before a word was uttered.

Larry Dressler, author of *Standing in the Fire*, says that in these moments of high heat, two kinds of energies ignite within us. One is the energy of reactivity and defensiveness, and the other is the energy of calm and deliberate choice.

Carol operated with calm and deliberate choice. She took pride in her ability to sense the wants and needs of the patients. I remember looking out into a filled waiting room with her. She gave a swift and accurate assessment of the emotional energy of the room with specific insight as to the patients' emotional and medical needs. Carol and Rebecca encountered the same tense situations every day. The difference was that Rebecca mentally set herself up for negative outcomes, and Carol poised herself for positive outcomes. You get more of whatever you focus on.

Now that you have awareness, you, too, can choose to be like Carol. Being clear about what you want affects others and allows you to anticipate situations and take appropriate action to ultimately get what you want.

A few years back, I was working with an executive who was really stuck in a negative pattern of thinking and behaving. It took three months of hard work, reminders, and reinforcement for him to get out of the ruts and create more productive neural pathways. It was not easy, but he would confirm that it was well worth it. The improvements in morale, productivity, and results were reasons enough, but he also experienced improvement in his personal relationships, especially with his kids. He says this is perhaps the most compelling reason to choose to make the change. Note the pivotal word here: "Choose." But choice does not equate to easy.

Why Is It So Hard?

Many internal factors can usurp our ability to maintain focus on what we want. And while these challenges are all going on inside, many outside factors poke and prod and clamor for our attention. Some we can control, and some we can't.

Here are nine primary factors that get in the way and make it difficult to change behavior.

Ruts in the Brain

It's hard to get out of ruts. I talked about driving in the winter on the interstate in South Dakota. The accumulated ice on the well-traveled roadways creates ruts that my car's tires always seem to settle into as I drive, almost like I'm operating on autopilot. Well-traveled pathways like these are also created in our brains. It is very difficult to get out of the path that is most traveled and the easiest to tread.

Unproductive Repetitive Behavior

What causes those ruts is the repetitive nature of our thoughts, actions, and behaviors. We like the sense of assurance that we know what's going to happen. We develop traditions such as holiday celebrations and habits such as driving the same route to work each day. But there are lots of things we do repetitively that are unproductive, such as nagging our kids to do chores or procrastinating on important projects.

Comfort Zone

We seek comfort, and familiarity breeds comfort. Even when we honestly reflect and recognize that certain actions and behaviors are not positive and are not serving us well, we continue to behave in the same way because we've been there. We feel a level of comfort with what is known and familiar. It is difficult to push outside that comfort zone.

Lack of Neuropathways

Most of us have limited neuropathways, or roadways, in our minds. Our experiences have programmed our brains with a small number of options for dealing with situations, and we handle them the same way or with only slight variations. What we need are multiple pathways that allow us to be far more flexible and agile. Without multiple pathways, our brains slide into familiar and well-traveled ruts. When we have multiple pathways in our brains, the process of changing and making changes is significantly easier.

Fear

We all have fears, and the most important thing we can do is acknowledge them. Fear is kind of like a virus on a computer. You can't really see it, and you often don't know what's causing it, but it's problematic. It's important to recognize what makes you fearful so you can deal with those fears. Important caveat: The advice here addresses typical fears that may be addressed with acknowledgment and actions, not psychological issues such as phobias, for which professional intervention is recommended.

Lack of Clarity

When people are not crystal clear about what they want, they do not know what they're aiming for. There is a tendency to say, "I want to be successful" or "I want to do well" or "I want this to work." These are vague statements that do not lend themselves to identifying specific action steps. Vague desires result in lack of direction and inaction.

Lack of Agility

Being stuck in ruts and trapped in repetitive activity greatly reduces agility. We're just letting things go along. It has never been more dangerous to allow this to keep happening. It hampers our ability to move and capture opportunities as they reveal themselves because we are so often on autopilot. We miss opportunities because we are asleep at the wheel.

Unproductive Relationship Habits

It is not uncommon that we hang around with people who make it a lot easier for us to stay with that old behavior and resist change. There is a powerful reason for very carefully selecting the people you hang around with. Conversing with others creates neuropathways in your brain. Synaptic connections may occur whether you are talking *or listening and observing*. A scientific experiment of mirror neurons demonstrated this fact: A device was attached to a monkey's brain. When the monkey picked up a peanut, there was an audible sound indicating that a neuroplastic connection (pathway between nerve cells) had occurred. Scientists repeated the experiment, and every time the monkey picked up the peanut, the audible sound was triggered. One day, one of the scientists reached over and picked up the peanut. When the monkey observed this, the audible sound occurred. This was a very interesting finding to the scientists. The monkey did not actually have to grab the peanut to create a synaptic connection. Just watching someone else grab it enabled a new neural pathway to form.

VUCA

This is an acronym borrowed from the Army War College. VUCA stands for volatility, uncertainty, complexity, and ambiguity. Bob Johansen, from the prestigious Institute for the Future, uses the acronym to describe the world in which we live and recommends ways we can proactively deal with these challenges. At the time this book is written, our current VUCA environment exacerbates people's natural tendency to remain safe and stick with what's familiar. But what we need is the opposite. This is a time when people need to be open to change and to take charge of their own behaviors—that is, operate with a *Seeing Red Cars* mind-set.

How Does This Apply to the Business World?

In times of dynamic change, as in the current marketplace, people tend to focus on what they don't want even more than normal because there are so many unknowns. People question how change will affect them and focus even more on what they don't want to have happen.

The way people respond to new information has a huge influence on the success of change initiatives in the workplace. As I mentioned at the beginning of this chapter, when people encounter important new information, they typically react in one of three ways: 20% are very open and excited about it, 50% are cautious and not forthcoming with their support, and 30% are openly opposed. Let's look at each:

20%   I call this group the ambassadors. It doesn't matter whether it's a business or a church group or a student association, 20% of the group will say, "Oh, my gosh, I have felt this. I have believed it, and I have personally developed this discipline. I didn't consciously know what it was, but now that you point out that this is a discipline, I recognize that it's a choice I have made. I'm so grateful. I want to be a part of it. I want to influence others. I want to help people, teams, and organizations not only be clear about what they want personally but also align with what we want for our team and for our organization."

50%   I call this group the fence-sitters. They can really understand it and intuitively recognize that it's there, but they're cautious and sensitive. They are more inclined to sit on the fence and observe. "Is there anything here? Is it really a big deal? Does it really matter?" They are not negative. They are not positive. They are neutral.

30%   This group is the detractors. They will say, "You've got to be kidding me." They'll find every reason why their thought process is valid and worthy. They will openly resist change.

When the ambassadors are interacting with the detractors, in reality they are talking "at" one another, not "with" one another.

They both work very hard at stating their case, but neither one truly listens. What commonly happens is that organizations focus a great deal of effort on convincing the detractors to change. Why? Because 30% is a lot of people and they are *vocal*. Frankly, the vast majority of the effort to sway the detractors is absolutely fruitless. Instead, the majority of the focus should be one-to-one conversations with the fence-sitters. When I'm working with organizations, I always ask, "Who are your ambassadors? Who are the most influential and trustworthy people within your organization who really want to be part of shifting the organizational culture?" Ask those ambassadors to reach out to the fence-sitters and begin the process of talking about how to align their personal wants with the organization's wants. These conversations are more about asking questions to alleviate concerns rather than telling people to just accept the new direction. Fence-sitters need to be invited to engage in the process and be part of the solution. Ambassadors can talk about the value of focusing on wants. It's all about questions. It's definitely not about telling. The power of engaging the 70%, the ambassadors and the fence-sitters, is where the greatest influence lies.

All the while, recognize that the detractors will be openly vocal while the organization is focusing on the 70%. To the detractors, the sheer notion of focusing on what we want and aligning our wants with the organization's vision, values, and desired outcomes is ludicrous. It sends them into a process of finding every reason why these things can't happen at this time. They will try to forge conversations with the ambassadors, which they quickly learn is a waste of time, and will actively try to convince the fence-sitters to join their team. As they say, misery loves company. Because the detractors are so vocal, organizations often fall into the trap of focusing on them (the squeaky wheel gets the grease). Don't do it. They are in the minority, and many of them will eventually come around. Continually feed positive messages and encouragement to the detractors, but don't openly engage in combat.

Another factor that is powerful and daunting during a time of change is that many people are simply unaware that their thinking is negative. Price Pritchett, a noted author and advisor to Fortune 500 companies, says, "Any time there is a major change, our first scan is for danger. That's just the way we're wired as a human being. It's a survival instinct. But too often people get hung up with what we call the five C's: complaining about the situation, criticizing management, commiserating with their colleagues, expressing their concern, and sometimes full-blown catastrophizing." And since about 70% of our thoughts are negative and "cruise through our consciousness undetected," he says people are in a poor position to correct the situation when only 30% of their thoughts are positive. That's where the *Seeing Red Cars* mind-set, if you have made it an intentional way that you operate, will spring into action and come to your aid. *Seeing Red Cars* is as much about focusing on what you want as it is about eliminating negative thoughts. Drive your actions toward positive outcomes by purposefully focusing on what you want instead of on what you are afraid of and trying to avoid. You get more of *whatever* you focus on.

The following story of two employees in the same organization beautifully illustrates the power of focusing on the 70% (ambassadors and fence-sitters). Carla was in the 50% group (fence-sitter), and George was in the 30% group (detractor) at an advanced biomedical company I was working with some years ago. The company established a very clear vision. I advised them to give their people a sight line to what is most important and to keep it visible and actionable. We developed a 12-week process to help people focus on the outcomes they were looking for. Every meeting began with "Here is where we are going, and here is where we are at. Where are each of you in this journey, and what steps are you going to take to close that gap?" That was their mode of operation.

Carla was an assembly-line worker and started out as a fence-sitter. She was very curious about the concepts, and frankly, they were a little unnerving to her. She cautiously began thinking to herself about her true passions, strengths, and values. When we were close to the end of the 12-week program, I noticed Carla wanted to speak to me after class. She hung back and waited to have a chance to talk. She finally approached me after everyone had left the room and told me her story. She found the *Seeing Red Cars* concept (focusing on what you want) intriguing, but it really scared her in the beginning. That was because she realized through the process that she really loves finance and numbers and she wanted to move into the accounting department. She gradually started talking about the idea with her colleagues and manager, and they encouraged her and gave her the confidence to focus on her true interests and values. She finally worked up the courage to apply for the accounting program at a local college. I had the opportunity to follow up with Carla over the years. She completed her accounting education and moved into the accounting department. Eventually, she moved into a leadership role in accounting before she moved to another organization when she married—you see, she had also identified the type of person she wanted to spend her life with during the original 12-week course and ultimately met that person and moved to another city, where she continued her journey as an accountant.

Now I'll tell you about George, in the same organization and going through the same 12-week program. He was the classic detractor. He squawked on and on. George talked about how it was ridiculous that focusing on outcomes could really have an impact on things and that being aware of the challenges and difficulties was far more important. He was absolutely resistant. Well, we didn't focus on George. We didn't leave him out, but we didn't focus on him. Over the course of three years, we created this thought process where it went from being cumbersome and uncomfortable in the beginning, like new things often are, to becoming very fluid and comfortable, where people were absolutely marching not only to their own personal "I want" statements but also to the statements, vision, and values of the organization.

I'll never forget the day when George, who had been defiant for so long, was leading a tour of the manufacturing facility. As George was standing in the hallway, I heard him saying, "The way that we operate here—the things that compel us, that get us up every morning, that have us wanting to get better day after day—is that we are truly guided by our vision. . . . That's not only the organization's vision, but each of us has clearly defined what we want to accomplish, and we are taking daily, weekly, and monthly actions to move toward those goals." That was three years into the project. When we heard George utter those words, we finally knew that we had made significant movement. I would venture to say that we had finally hit critical mass. But let me once again reinforce this point. We didn't push George. Early efforts, early conversations, were absolutely futile. Instead, we put our energies and our effort into the 20% who were really aligned with the thought process, the ambassadors, and into the 50% who were more cautious, the fence-sitters. And lo and behold, we were able to really influence everyone down to the most vocal detractors and to create a culture that absolutely supported focusing on the desired outcomes.

CHAPTER 2

Rewire Your Brain for Better Outcomes

Recognizing that there is scientific proof the brain can be changed can heighten your awareness and begin the process of understanding and applying this knowledge. Start looking for ways to intentionally change your mind and create the large and small outcomes you desire. This is important: This type of change is *not* a step-by-step process; it is a dynamic process requiring constant awareness, and you must keep working at it with diligence and persistence. You must keep practicing the new behaviors in situations large and small. This chapter revisits those nine factors that make it difficult to change behavior with an eye toward strategies you can use to literally rewire your brain and create better outcomes.

Overcome Ruts in the Brain by Building New Roads

Getting out of well-trod ruts requires creating multiple pathways in our brains. We need to engage in new and different activities to get out of our comfortable patterns.

The analogy I often use is this: Imagine you're in your car in Small Town A. You're on Main Street. When you want to go to Small Town B, you typically have two choices: Drive one way or the opposite way on Main Street, and you're out of town quickly.

You've done it hundreds of times. You don't try other routes because you know that these two will get you where you need to go. What if a new side road recently opened that cuts 10 minutes of drive time to Small Town B, but you haven't heard about it yet? You would not venture down that road when you need to go to Small Town B because you know that going north on Main Street will get you there. Eventually, word spreads that a new road to Small Town B has opened. You try it the next time you need to go there. You now know three ways to get out of Small Town A, and you add the new route to the options catalogued in your brain.

Now you're in a large city, and you need to drive out of the city. On one road, you encounter road construction, so you turn onto another road. The next road has a train passing over it, blocking your way. You'll probably take another turn and reroute where you were going to go. There are many roads you can choose. Once you find one that leads you out of the city, you make a mental note of the street and the landmarks so you can find it again. Large cities have multiple roads leading in and out, and you can test new routes over time and discover which ones get you to your destinations with the least potential for roadblocks. They all get catalogued in your brain and give you greater flexibility to avoid delays. Likewise, when we have multiple pathways in our brains, the process of changing and making changes is significantly easier.

Create Productive New Behaviors

Once new pathways have been created, we need to repeat the new behaviors to gain comfort and assurance. Driving a different way out of a city may have worked that one time when road construction forced us to try a new route, but we know the usual route is the one we're most familiar with. Unless the alternate route proves to be faster or almost always less congested, we'll revert back to the familiar behavior. Once we try the alternate route a few times, we start to remember landmarks and discover a few other ways to connect up with the alternate route. It now becomes our secret back door to exiting the city during rush hour. The additional routes we learn add greater flexibility to our commute.

Ease out of Comfort Zones by Taking It S-L-O-W

Most of the time when we identify what we want, we are moving outside our comfort zones. Mary may want better results from team meetings than just sitting and listening. She decides she wants to contribute at least one useful idea in every meeting. She has never spoken up before. The goal in this situation is to create a stretch—a small stretch, not a huge one. Trying to force changes too quickly ignites the amygdala and the emotional response associated with fear and concern, and it releases cortisol, which shuts down learning, focus, and creativity.

Here's a story that illustrates the process:

Barbara advanced to a new position where she was often going to be speaking to groups. I was teaching two programs on high-impact presentations at the time. One was a 12-week course that broke down the process and guided participants along at a steady pace. This was a great starting point for most people. The other was a two-day workshop where we briefly covered the process of preparing for the presentation and did a little bit of prep work, and then the learners practiced presenting in front of the group numerous times while being videotaped.

Barbara's company enrolled her in the two-day workshop. When she arrived, it became immediately obvious that even the process of being in the group was outside her comfort zone. When Barbara stepped in front of the group to speak, her physiological response to the experience was obvious on every level. She broke out in a cold sweat, and then this welt worked its way up her neck and ultimately covered her entire face by the time she was finished speaking. It was absolutely painful to watch.

We contacted her organization and said we felt she would do better in the 12-week course. As often happens, the company wanted things to get better quickly because they did not feel they had the time to put her through a 12-week program. They said she was ready and wanted her to stay in the two-day workshop. We had a conversation with her. She said she was willing to stay, but things didn't improve. Over the course of two days, every single time she spoke, she was clearly outside her comfort zone. There was no way that she was able to grow through the experience. Her natural response to fear kicked in and triggered her amygdala, which shut down creativity and innovation. The organization tried to force her into change too quickly.

Create More Pathways in Your Brain by Doing New and Different Things

The amygdala gets spooked easily. Small steps forge new pathways in your brain that allow you to retrain the amygdala. This releases serotonin, which allows you to respond with creativity, innovation, and focus. New things you can try include taking a new way home from work, learning a new skill or avocation, or seeking counsel from someone who looks at a situation in a new and different way.

Take Action to Overcome Fears

Acknowledge that you have fears, and recognize the things that cause negative reactions to those fears. Call it out and acknowledge it because once you recognize it's there and call it out, you can take decisive action to move in a more positive direction.

What causes you to be fearful? I know that for me, the things that cause fear are boredom and the pressure to conform or to be roped into mundane activity. Those are the types of things that cause me to feel fearful and anxious and react in a way that I'm not really proud of.

You have the power to set your own GPS (Global Positioning System) for interesting projects, great people, real collaboration, innovation, and more. It really comes down to forging new pathways in your brain.

Counter Lack of Clarity by Being Specific about What You Want

When people have a great deal of clarity about what they want and they know what they are aiming for, they do the things that move them down that road. Instead of just saying "I want to be successful," they write down the answers to questions like these: What does success look like? Who do I want to work with? Who are my target clients? What are my target projects? What will those projects look like when they're completed? How will I work with others along the way? What will the dynamics be? How will I address challenges? In what ways will I provide feedback or will feedback be provided?

Answers to questions like these help us establish the clarity we need. Ultimately, when we have that type of clarity, it's a lot easier to take action.

Visualize Ideal Outcomes to Increase Agility

When you are very clear about what you want, you picture the outcomes in your mind, and when you engage in taking actions toward your goals, you will be far more agile. Here is an exercise I often use:

Brian has an important meeting coming up. The stakes are high, and the outcome is unknown. To help him prepare, I ask Brian to pretend that the meeting has already taken place and was very successful. I keep asking questions until Brian can describe the meeting in great detail. I ask him:

1. What are the participants thinking? He says, "They are thinking that the subject matter was fully discussed in a very logical manner. They are thinking they have enough information to make decisions about the next steps. They are thinking about their next steps."

2. What are the participants feeling? "They are feeling confident and are ready to take action to move the project along. They feel that their concerns were heard and addressed proactively."

3. What are you thinking? "I'm glad I listened first and then shared our findings later. I'm thinking it was very helpful to address questions and concerns and to also keep the conversation focused on the subject. And I'm glad I incorporated their views into the recommendations."

4. What are you feeling? "I am feeling confident and committed to the project."

Brian's answers served as a powerful guide as he entered the meeting. During the meeting, something was said by a participant that was not taken in the way that Brian had hoped. At this point, Brian had such a clear expectation of what was going to happen and what everyone was thinking and feeling that he sprang into action. Brian told me, "We addressed the participants' questions and concerns in a systematic manner. We kept the conversation focused on the subject and successfully redirected communication when it began to stray off subject. We solicited ideas for action on the project and were able to share our findings and recommendations while incorporating the thoughts and ideas of all participants, leaving everyone feeling involved and integral to the project's success."

Brian was able to bring the meeting around to a positive place. By operating from this position of intention, serotonin was released inside Brian's brain, and he responded with creativity and innovation on the spot.

For yourself, recognize the value and importance of agility and creating more and more pathways in your brain so that you, like Brian, will operate from a standpoint of greater clarity. You will make shifts easily in actual situations because you have been there before in your mind.

Create Productive Relationship Habits by Associating with Forward-Thinking People

Hang around with people who have very positive thinking. Recognize the power of mirror neurons; remember the monkey whose synaptic connections were triggered whether he picked up the peanut or watched the scientist pick it up. Your mind takes in information, whether positive or negative, from the people you hang around with. You observe what they're talking about, how they respond to situations, and everything else about them. Be careful that they are the kind of people who will forge desirable pathways in your brain.

Create Positive Outcomes in a VUCA Environment

To combat VUCA—volatility, uncertainty, complexity, and ambiguity—Bob Johansen of the Institute for the Future says that you need understanding and awareness of what is going on in the marketplace. Have a clear vision and know what you want personally and professionally for yourself, your team, and the organization. Remember the *Seeing Red Cars* reality: You get more of *whatever* you focus on. When you operate with curiosity and a desire to learn and understand, you remain open to new ideas. It allows you to maneuver better in a VUCA environment and create positive outcomes. Those who operate effectively despite VUCA will be infinitely more successful.

Change Is Hard Work

Causing change takes hard work because you're asking your brain to forge new pathways that have not yet been established. I like to use this story to illustrate the point: Right before Christmas last year, we got about 10 inches of snow in Minnesota. I was excited because I love snowshoeing—strapping the big tennis-racket-size footwear on your boots so you can walk on top of the snow (snowshoes distribute your weight over a larger area so your feet do not sink completely into the snow). I strapped on my snowshoes and started to walk—trudge, more like. There was no path yet, so it took extra effort. Step after intentional step. Even though it was cold outside, I quickly started to sweat. I took off my jacket. I kept thinking to myself, Why don't I turn back now? It was hard work. The next day I went out, it was a lot less challenging. Snowshoeing was still difficult because the path was not yet well formed, but it required a little less effort than the first day. The third day, it became less challenging because I had already been down that path a couple of times. By the time I'd been down that path four or five times, it was not really difficult at all.

Before taking action when new information is introduced, understand which group you are in:

20%   Believe in focusing on what you want. Excited about it. Totally on board.

50%   Neutral. It makes sense that focusing on what you want is best, but you're not totally sold on the idea.

30%   Totally resistant. You don't get it. This is a bunch of hooey.

If you're in one of the first two groups and you want to try to influence the behavior of others, it is important to recognize which groups they are in because people have to want to change. I remember being very young when I recognized that my mom was in the 30% group (a detractor). She focused on what she didn't want, and she got a *lot* more of it. If she approached a door with a key in her hand, she would be saying to herself, "I bet I will turn the key in the wrong direction" or "I won't be able to figure out how to work it." And then, lo and behold, she would not be able to get the key to work. Invariably, someone would step in to turn the key with ease, and she'd look away with this pained look on her face and mutter some form of self-loathing under her breath. Early on, I found the process painful, but it didn't take long to recognize that she was bringing it on herself. I tried in my youthful and innocent ways to help her see the light. I was never able to get through.

Naively, at 23, I wrote what I thought was a powerful letter of encouragement and inspiration. I felt that she could be happier and was capable of so many things, and I was determined to help her recognize that the solution was pretty simple. After sending the letter, I waited for her call. It didn't come. When I reached out to her, she addressed the letter straightforwardly. "This is who I am," she said. "I'm quite used to being disappointed with outcomes in my life and, frankly, I don't want to change." She was kind and sweet. It was not a confrontational moment. It was a telling one.

We all know and care about people whose thoughts and behaviors create circumstances that are not positive. We have to recognize that people need to come to these realizations on their own terms and in their own time—and that some never will.

How Does This Apply to the Business World?

When I talk to people who are in the 20% group (ambassadors) or the 50% group (fence-sitters), they recognize the natural tendency for people to focus on what they don't want, and when they go back to work, they suddenly realize there is so much of this going on. They become extremely aware of it. People all around them are focusing on what they don't want. They recognize it is prevalent and damaging, and they really feel a need to turn things around because they know this negative mind-set is getting in the way. That's when frustration kicks in because, as you know, "You can lead a horse to water but you can't make him drink." People have to *want* to change.

In these situations, I advise people to create signs and signals for themselves (i.e., Red Cars memory triggers) that act as reminders to focus on what they want. Think of it this way: When you're driving down the road, you encounter periodic road signs. These signs remind you of the speed limit and let you know that you're on the right road. What you need in your personal life is some kind of visual or emotional trigger that jogs your memory when you encounter new and different situations. You can be going along focusing on what you want until something unexpected pops up. In those situations, whatever you pick as your personal road sign (a vision of a red car? the good feelings you have when you accomplish a desired outcome? the picture in your mind of what a successful meeting looks and feels like?) must pop into your mind and jog your memory of what you want to have happen. Find ways to create those kinds of reminders for yourself. Like the road signs, they will let you know that you're on the right track, and you'll respond in a positive manner.

The beauty of the *Seeing Red Cars* metaphor is the abundance of red objects you can use as visual, auditory, or tactile triggers. (See the triggers section in the back of this book for ideas.) Wear red clothing, place red objects in your workspace, use Red Cars screen savers or cell phone applications, or even buy a red car! Many people build a long-term program with Red Cars cues and events (e.g., video stories, group activities) to extend the experience and keep the concepts in front of them. With constant awareness aided by Red Cars memory joggers, you *will* rewire your brain and cause the outcomes you desire.

Play to Your Strengths and Control What You Can

Success with the *Seeing Red Cars* mind-set all begins with knowing yourself. If you know what you're passionate about and what really interests you, and you know your strengths, they are yours; *they are your intellectual property.* You can take them anywhere. What trips people up is the challenge of *maintaining intentional focus* on their passions, interests, and strengths. If you don't call them out, recognize them, and act on them with intention, your natural tendency to slip back into thinking about what you fear and are trying to avoid will reign. Remember, you get more of *whatever* you focus on.

Start with the knowledge of your passions, interests, and strengths, and then pay close, constant attention to what you *can* control, along with what you want and are working toward. Create for yourself mental pictures of your desired outcomes and the feelings associated with achieving those wants, and choose red objects or items to remind you of those desired outcomes. In other words, keep *Seeing Red Cars.* At those times when your positive outcomes mind-set is challenged, picture your Red Cars memory joggers in your mind and snap back into awareness and action. You can do it. It works.

Play to Your Strengths

What commonly happens is that people complete high school, go on to college, and enter the working world. The pressures of paying bills, starting families, and climbing the career ladder cause them to accept opportunities that do not play to their passions, interests, and strengths. Now they feel trapped. But it's never too late to reevaluate and focus on what truly drives you.

Corporate America has long valued the employee who can do many things. This causes people to build their professional muscles in every way possible. But when people are not doing work that is interesting, that does not tap their strengths, and that is not enjoyable, it's like pushing an elephant up the stairs.

Playing to our strengths is just the opposite. It brings out the best in us. It's the kind of work we get lost in. When we are trying to be everything to everyone, it's easy to end up down the path that keeps us busy and pays the bills but yields little satisfaction and drains us.

What Are Your Strengths?

It's important to flesh out your passions and strengths. For some, the word *passion* is a bit strong. You may be more comfortable with the term *interest*. So, what are you passionate about or what really interests you? When you're doing work that you're passionate about, you lose track of time and you're filled with energy. Look for times and activities in which you lost yourself. Reflect back on your life, even back to your youth. What were you passionate about, and what were you interested in? Knowing this is the place to start. If you don't know it just yet, stick with it until it reveals itself to you. With the right determination, study, and conversation, you'll figure it out.

How do you recognize a strength? For starters, it comes easily for you. In fact, it probably comes so easy you take it for granted.

We often overlook and underestimate the good that we can do when we are playing to our passions and strengths. It takes a lot less effort than other things, and it brings the best of ourselves to the project or challenge. It's exactly what organizations need today.

Before I take you through the Red Cars Toolkit to map your personal strengths and "I wants," I'll show you a completed example for Joe, an accountant who has been working for five years. He completed the following "Personal" activities from the Red Cars Toolkit:

Tool 1. Passions/Interests and Strengths

Tool 2. Passions/Interests, Strengths, and Values

Tool 3. Bucket List

Tool 4. Well-Rounded Wheel

Tool 5. Well-Rounded "I Want" Statements

Tool 6. Bridge Worksheet

At this time, just review Joe's example before you begin. I will provide instructions next.

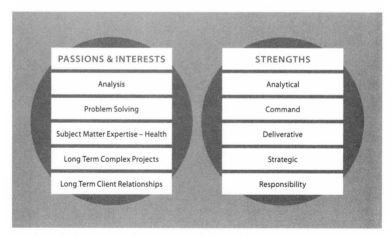

Tool 1 Joe's Passions/Interests and Strengths

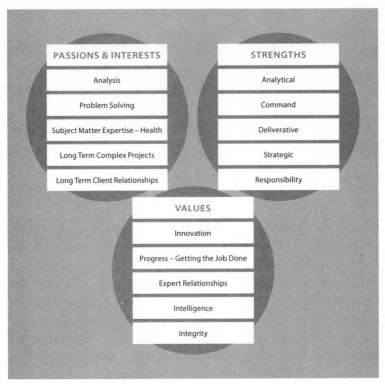

Tool 2 Joe's Passions/Interests, Strengths, and Values

BUCKET LIST
for a well-rounded me

What I want...

- I want to do work which is interesting and challenging to me.
- I want to be a manager by the time I am 30 years old.
- I want to work for a company that has a mission I believe in.
- I want to consistently contribute the maximum % to my investment account.
- Beyond the company 401K I want to invest a further 10% of my income.
- I want to consistently work out 3 days per week.
- I want to run a marathon.
- I want to learn how to cook healthy food.
- I want to have a small group of good friends.
- I want to marry my best friend and then spend my life with her.
- I want to have a family and put them first in my life.
- I want to travel to Italy.
- I want to go to one sports or music event each month.
- I want to do volunteer work each month.

Tool 3   Joe's Bucket List

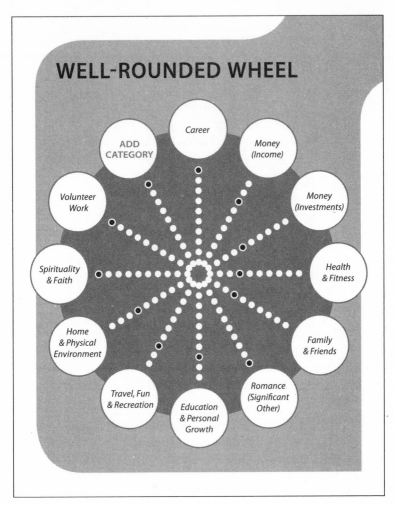

Tool 4 Joe's Well-Rounded Wheel
Note the position of the black dots. The center of the wheel is zero, and the perimeter is 10.

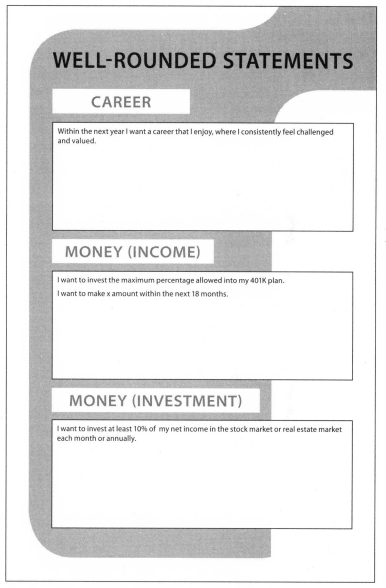

WELL-ROUNDED STATEMENTS

CAREER

Within the next year I want a career that I enjoy, where I consistently feel challenged and valued.

MONEY (INCOME)

I want to invest the maximum percentage allowed into my 401K plan.

I want to make x amount within the next 18 months.

MONEY (INVESTMENT)

I want to invest at least 10% of my net income in the stock market or real estate market each month or annually.

Tool 5 Joe's Well-Rounded "I Want" Statements

BRIDGE TO A WELL-ROUNDED YOU

Where I/we are:

I make x a year

I do not invest above and beyond my 401K

I work out sporadically and am in pathetic shape.

I do not get out much! I don't plan and consequently time just seems to skip by.

I like technology but feel the need to increase my skills

What I/we want:

I want to make x amount within the next 18 months. (Money-Income)

I want to invest at least 10% of my income in the stock market or real estate market each month. (Money-Investment)

I want to lift weights twice a week and do cardio exercise 3 times a week (Health/Fitness)

I want to plan 1 special family/friend activity a month. (Family/Friends)

I want to read one book a month. (Education/Personal Growth)

Must Haves:

I want to make x amount within the next 18 months. (Money-Income)

I want to lift weights twice a week and do cardio exercise 3 times a week (Health/Fitness)

I want to plan 1 special family/friend activity a month. (Family/Friends)

Nice, but not necessary:

I want to invest at least 10% of my income in the stock market or real estate market each month. (Money-Investment)

I want to read one book a month. (Education/Personal Growth)

Tool 6   Joe's Bridge Worksheet

Now that you've seen Joe's example, you can complete the activities for yourself. The first step is to identify your greatest strengths. In my line of work, I have had the good fortune to use numerous assessment tools that have been tested through exhaustive analyses of tens of thousands of people. They help people pinpoint their greatest strengths and align those with their passions and interests. They have helped people recast their futures. If you would like to complete an assessment, I recommend Tom Rath's *StrengthsFinder 2.0* and Marcus Buckingham and Donald Clifton's *Now, Discover Your Strengths*.

Buckingham and researchers at the Gallup organization analyzed the results of interviews conducted with more than 1.7 million employees from 101 companies representing 63 countries. When asked, only 20% said they are using their strengths daily. Granted, adults recognize that they will not enjoy what they are doing 100% of the time. They know that work is work, not a day at the amusement park. I've found that if people are doing work they are passionate about or interested in, and are playing to their strengths, 60% of the time they will evaluate their work experience positively. But if it falls short of 60%, even just a little bit short, the grass will most certainly look greener elsewhere, and they will begin looking for other opportunities or else psychologically check out, revert to autopilot, and seek gratification in other areas of their lives.

You might feel that you already know your strengths, but I still encourage you to complete an assessment. It will provide insight that will guide you. Once you know your strengths, you can leverage them. You will be able to more easily and clearly articulate how your strengths will serve the project, your team, and the company. Everybody wins.

Following are the steps to complete the Red Cars activities.

RED CARS Toolkit

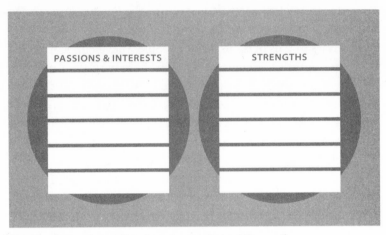

Tool 1   Record your Passions/Interests and Strengths

Download the Red Cars Toolkit PDF from www.seeingred-carsbook.com. (Your answers will automatically be populated on the subsequent pages where the categories appear.) Enter words that you feel best describe your greatest strengths. The 34 themes and ideas from *StrengthsFinder 2.0* might help:

Achiever: You are in constant need of achievement.

Activator: You want to know, "When can we start?"

Adaptability: You respond willingly to the demands of the moment.

Analytical: You think, "Prove it. Show me why what you're claiming is true."

Arranger: When faced with a complex situation involving many factors, you enjoy managing all the variables.

Belief: You have core values that are enduring.

Command: You prefer to lead and take charge.

Communication: You like to explain, to describe, to host, to speak in public, and to write.

Competition: When you look at the world, you compare. Others' performance is the ultimate yardstick. And when you win, there is no feeling quite like it.

Connectedness: You feel that things happen for a reason. You are considerate, caring, and accepting.

Consistency: Balance is important to you. You are keenly aware of the need to treat people the same, no matter what their station in life or in the organization.

Context: You look back because that is where the answers lie.

Deliberative: You are careful. You are vigilant.

Developer: You see the potential in others.

Discipline: Your world needs to be predictable.

Empathy: You can sense the emotions of others around you.

Focus: You need a clear destination that guides your actions.

Futuristic: You are the kind of person who loves to peer over the horizon.

Harmony: You look for areas of agreement.

Ideation: You are fascinated by ideas.

Includer: You want to include people and make them feel part of the group.

Individualization: You are intrigued by the unique qualities of each person.

Input: You are inquisitive.

Intellection: You like to think. You like mental activity.

Learner: You love to learn.

Maximizer: You like to transform something strong into something superb.

Positivity: You are generous with praise, quick to smile, and always on the lookout for the positive in a situation.

Relator: You are drawn toward people you already know.

Responsibility: You are bound to follow through to completion anything you commit to.

Restorative: You love to solve problems.

Self-Assurance: You have faith in your strengths.

Significance: You want to be very significant in the eyes of other people.

Strategic: You are able to sort through the clutter and find the best route.

Woo: You are good at winning others over.

Under Passions & Interests, enter words that describe what you are passionate about or have a strong interest in, such as helping others, adventure, or solving complex problems. Maybe it's faith, teaching, or public speaking. Focus on what gets *your* heart racing.

Once you identify what drives you—your personal passions, interests, and strengths—it becomes easier to stay true to these guides and to respond to situations and the choices you face. The following story about Billy McLaughlin is an incredible example of the power of choice, even against what first appears to be an insurmountable obstacle, to stay true to personal strengths and to ultimately succeed.

When life throws curveballs, those who not only survive but thrive are the ones who remain focused on what they want and what they *can* control. They may need to take some time for sorrow and grief, but then they pick themselves up, dust off, and start focusing on the things they can do to get themselves back on track.

I interviewed Billy for the TV show *Life to the Max*. For 20 years, in the 1980s and 1990s, Billy was commanding the attention of thousands. He was an internationally recognized guitarist and composer and was considered to be the musician's musician. His performances were solo, and the attention was all on him. All of a sudden, two fingers on his right hand, his dominant hand, began to curl without reason. For three years, he desperately sought answers to what was going on. He saw every physician and every specialist he could find. No one could explain it. Finally, he went to the Sister Kenny Institute in Minneapolis, Minnesota, for an examination by Jeanine Speier, who told him, "Billy, you have focal dystonia." It is an incurable neuromuscular disease that affects people in different ways. In Billy's case, it affected two fingers on his dominant hand. Dr. Speier looked at Billy and said, "I believe it's time to find another profession." This message sent Billy into a downward spiral for a time. He was distraught. But one morning he woke up and said to himself, "I can focus on what I can't control, or I can focus on what I *can* control."

What Billy had going for him was a fan base and a proven market for his work. The only things that had changed were two fingers on his dominant hand. He still had his fully functioning left hand, his inborn musical gifts, and a willingness to work at reinventing himself. He said to himself, "I can't control this disease, and I know that there's no treatment for it. But what I can control is the left side of my body." Billy began a quest to relearn how to play his music left-handed, on his nondominant side. It is akin to learning how to speak the language—every word in your vocabulary—backward. So Billy closed himself in a room and began to practice. Here was a musician who had commanded the attention of thousands, in a room playing on his nondominant side "Mary Had a Little Lamb" extremely badly. I asked him in the interview, "Billy, what did you learn from this experience?" He said, "I learned how to be comfortable being really bad because no matter what it is, when you're learning something new, you're going to be really bad to begin with."

This part of the interview really sticks out in my mind because it is exactly the message that I tell people who are resistant to change. I say, "When you experience adversity, if you have the ability to focus your mind on what you can control, and what you want, it will almost certainly be extremely difficult at first, and you will probably start off being really bad at whatever new thing you are trying to do, but stick with it. It will take some time, but you, like Billy, will gradually become fluid and comfortable and confident in even the most challenging of situations. You will land on your feet."

Now, in 2010, at the time of this writing, Billy is back. He is playing at the level, if not better than, he did prior to focal dystonia. He retrained his mind to overcome this incredible obstacle. Now he is not only the phenomenal musician he was before his health condition, his amazing success story has become a role model for others.

This need to adapt and shift gears also occurs in organizations. Unfortunately, it doesn't matter how much you love the work you have done in the past or how successful it made you yesterday. When the marketplace changes, you must shift gears and build muscle where there currently is fat, or you perish! Better start lifting weights.

I recently had a conversation with a partner at a highly successful design firm. The leader said, "The way we connect with our clients has changed. Our old methods no longer yield the results they once did, and the tools and technologies available allow the folks down the street to show their wares to clients in ways that are highly interactive and very real. This is very appealing to clients. We have a firm that is filled with some of the city's finest designers, but our methods of communication and the tools we have always employed to bring our clients' visions to life are antiquated and cause us to look unkempt and out of step. If we are to successfully maneuver into the future, we will have to cast a new vision that will require a shift in our thinking and mastering new technologies and tools." Like Billy McLaughlin, if the people in the design firm love their craft enough, they will have to be comfortable being really bad at first and commit to working long and hard to bridge the gap between where they are now and where they need to be. It's likely to be awkward and not terribly fun for a spell. This is true with many people, teams, and organizations. What once worked no longer works, and the shift in gears will be challenging. But please *do* shift. We need you.

So think to yourself, what do I love so much that I'm willing to drive that extra mile? What am I willing to be uncomfortable and awkward at doing in the early stages, knowing that with practice and persistence I will become fluid, comfortable, confident— and extremely happy?

What Can You Control?

When I speak to groups about change, I refer to the ability to be change-adaptive. I like to give the example of New York. When you arrive in New York, you often feel like "If I could just slow these people down, everything would be all right." But anyone who has been to New York knows that you just have to pick up your pace and move at the same rate as the people around you, and soon you get into the rhythm.

Another way to look at this is having the ability to go with the flow. I tell a story of when I was a kid and we had a small creek on our property. One spring was particularly rainy, and the water had swelled well beyond the creek's banks. The creek had become a massive body of water. I was walking at the edge of it, and the current swept my feet from beneath me. I was swimming, frantically, against the current. My dad was by the side of the water and yelled, "Laura! Turn! Swim with the current! Turn now!" He was shouting as he was running at the water's edge in the direction the current was flowing. Finally, I turned with the current and began to swim with it, and then I was able to swim to the side of the shore.

I told these two stories in a presentation to a group of engineers. At the end of the talk, an engineer approached and told me his story. John had been leading a project for his former employer. He said he took a great deal of pride in the project. One day a leader in the organization announced that a part of their business was going away. It wasn't changing; it was absolutely going away. It was his project. At that point, he said, he literally fell apart. "In that moment, I lost my soul," he told me.

After the announcement was made, John looked around the room and saw that others were reacting to the situation, too, but most of them were not reacting in the dramatic way that he was. He thought to himself, "They are so fortunate to have been given that gift, the ability to change and adapt like they are. I so wish I would have gotten it." He felt that he was unable to change. He ended up losing his job. Another engineer who had a leadership role on the project was placed on a new project and moved on effortlessly.

John said that eventually he realized he did have a choice. "What I needed to do was to go with the flow. Others didn't have a gift, per se; they had made a choice." Had John reacted favorably, he would have been placed on another project like his colleague was. John said he learned the lesson the hard way, and he would never again be left behind. He learned that he had a choice. He just didn't pick the right one.

The moral of this story is that it has never been more important for us to be change-adaptive than it is right now, in this environment of dynamic change. Stay focused on what you want, and go with the flow. Act on what you *can* control.

What Do You Want Right Now?

Even teaching the *Seeing Red Cars* mind-set does not automatically equate to using it. When David Chard was leading an annual regional academy in Bangkok for Edelman, an international public relations firm, he experienced his own Red Car moment and had to have his memory jarred into action by his assistant.

The academy had been conducted for five years, and its focus was on leading mind-sets. On the first day, Chard opens with an awareness exercise so participants can experience how the mind filters information. He explains that when the mind's unconscious filter is focused on the negative—or what you don't want—you inevitably get more of that. But when it's consciously focused on what you *do* want, and your awareness is on the here and now, then the result of getting what you do want is more easily realized.

He shows the film *Seeing Red Cars* and uses discussions and activities to help participants see how they can use the Red Cars notion in their business and in their daily experiences in their offices. From time to time, Red Car moments occur when people inevitably get stuck, and he helps the group acknowledge what's happening and then revisit their "I want" statements. "Awareness gives you the opportunity to intervene in it," says Chard.

The whole concept of leading mind-sets is the belief that leaders need to be conscious people, explains Chard. "Mastery in anything goes far beyond merely 'knowing' about something. When you are able to do something unconsciously, without thinking about it, then you have mastery. This ability comes from doing something repeatedly until the unconscious mind takes over from the conscious mind and allows things to simply 'flow' when they are needed."

The best part of this story is that in 2010 the real learning happened outside the actual academy. Chard explained, "We had 66 people flying to Bangkok for one week for the academy." Upon arrival, Chard and a few of his staff members went to retrieve their preshipped materials from customs. The customs officials were concerned about something and denied the request to release the boxes. All of the materials for the academy were in those boxes. They tried unsuccessfully to reason with the customs officials. Nothing worked. Finally, Chard sat down in frustration. The academy was scheduled to begin in a matter of hours, and they had no materials. They felt defeated. After a few minutes, his assistant turned to him and said, "David, we have to focus on what we want right now. What do we want?" At that very moment, he explained, they all became completely resourceful. They got the approval. They went into town. They found the resources that they needed to make T-shirts, copy the materials, and create the welcome bags and everything else they needed to do the *Seeing Red Cars* High Potential Leadership Academy. Chard said that once they changed their thinking, they were able to immediately come up with innovative solutions to turn the situation around.

Moments of stress and moments of change are ideal situations to jog your mind back to awareness. Catch yourself before your emotions get the best of you. These are the times when the natural tendency to focus on what you don't want typically bubbles up to the surface and consumes you. Knowing how you behave and how you respond to stress gives you the awareness you need to deal with these situations.

Taking "I Wants" to the Team and Organizational Levels

When change occurs or you're confronted with a stressful event, you need to immediately respond, "What do I want?" Again, the critical question you have to ask is "What *can* I control?" John, the engineer, could not control the fact that his pet project was going away, but he could control his reaction to it. We need to create paved pathways in our brains so that when we encounter a change, when there is a fork in the road, our minds immediately go to the place of solutions, innovations, creativity, focus, and learning. For David Chard and his staff in Bangkok, all of those assets immediately arose for them once they made that shift. It is easy to see in these stories how this applies to individuals. We need to go further and also apply these principles to teams and ultimately to organizations.

Caution: It is crucial to implement the Red Cars mind-set in the context of what is going on in the marketplace. Your focus on what you want personally must take into account what is going on around you. And today's marketplace is chaotic. Uncertainty is rampant, which makes the natural tendency to focus on what we don't want even more pervasive.

Organizations of the future must understand and communicate what their vision is—what they want—but as demands change, they also must adapt to the market so they can successfully maneuver the wild curves in the road ahead. Consider for a moment if people at all levels of an organization are operating with a sight line to the company's top priorities, coupled with the personal discipline to focus on what they can control and what they want. Contrast that environment with one in which people are just doing their jobs and not particularly in tune with the company's or their department's goals and objectives. Now interject a major marketplace shift or the closure of a large division. The latter group will be sent into a tailspin, with people hovering around the water cooler or in cyber discussions in utter chaos and shock, while employees in the former company will respond with resourcefulness and pivot to create the next opportunity. It's a matter of discipline, planning, and deliberate choice.

Organizations that make this shift—to being focused on and disciplined in engaging and connecting individuals' "wants" with organizational "wants" while being keenly aware of marketplace needs and changes—are more likely to succeed.

A great example is the transformation—or, rather, the adaptation—of the Deluxe Corporation, founded in 1915 in St. Paul,

Minnesota. I suspect that most people reading this book can associate the name Deluxe with checkbooks. Remember the days before cash cards and credit cards? Our family could literally write 5 to 15 checks *per day* for every purchase we made. I still have piles of canceled checks returned from the bank in my basement. Nowadays, we all use online banking, online bill pay, and cash and credit cards for purchases.

According to an article written by Deluxe Chief Experience Officer Marti Woods, the company experienced a period of bottom-up innovation in the early 1990s. Deluxe account representatives who were servicing the old printed-check accounts started noticing that more of their clients were asking questions not about checks, but about how to attract and retain customers and increase loyalty in the financial services industry. More account reps were picking up on this pattern and realized it was something that deserved more attention. Deluxe's executive leadership gave the concept room to grow, and today the Customer Experience Division is generating revenue by charging banks and credit unions subscription fees to access its knowledge base. The company has expanded to offering graphic design and other advertising and promotional services to the same large, long-term client base it built through its printed-check business.

For Deluxe to survive, it had to adapt. Marketplace shifts required the company to shift gears and develop competency and product offerings aligned with marketplace needs. People still use paper checks, and the company is still the leader in that segment. But its business has dramatically shifted to focus on small business services and financial services. Many organizations will be required to make radical changes like this in the future. And those organizations will need employees who are able to shift gears quickly if they are to survive. A fully engaged workforce will be required to scan the horizon for shifts and changes, and its members must be skilled at focusing on what they can control and what they want in light of the changing marketplace.

CHAPTER 4

Tune in and Take Charge

Staying up-to-date on the changes going on around you plays a significant role in your ability to steer your life in a direction that leverages your strengths and interests. Success with the *Seeing Red Cars* mind-set requires you to constantly seek and remain open to new information while paying conscious attention to life's road signs—steering toward opportunities, such as technology that allows you to connect, communicate, and learn differently, and away from hazards, such as negative people, that you encounter along the way. I call it *Seeing Red Cars* while intentionally driving with high beams on. When you operate this way automatically, you will be well equipped for those times when a change occurs or a tragedy strikes that causes you to have to turn the wheel in a different direction. You will control your own destiny.

You will be glad you completed the exercises in this book and are commanding your own direction, as you will be prepared to respond proactively to workplace changes. Don Tapscott, coauthor of *Wikinomics* and *Macrowikinomics*, says, "There is a fundamental change taking place in terms of how corporations create value, and, arguably, in terms of the core architecture of the corporation. I think it's the biggest change in a century in the ways that companies build relationships and interact with other entities, institutions in the economy and in society. We are in the early days of this fundamental change and we need to reboot business and the world." Businesses themselves are paying closer attention and driving with intention and high beams on. Be ready to assert yourself appropriately. Employees at all levels need to engage and be a part of the solutions.

To effect positive change and make it stick, be keenly aware of and curious about marketplace dynamics and trends so you can steer your thoughts, actions, and learning in ways that are relevant and valuable. One of the easiest ways to do this is to engage technology. Social media is a gateway to the fabulous storehouse of information in the virtual world. This chapter also addresses the importance of talking with as many people as possible about your potential career direction, utilizing supporters, and dealing effectively with the doubters you encounter along the way.

Leverage Technology

In 1994, the Minneapolis–St. Paul *Star Tribune* ran a four-part series titled "On the Edge of the Digital Age," by Peter Leyden. At the time, the Internet was new, and cell phones were in their infancy. The series predicted the environment we live in today in which we connect, communicate, and learn in large measure by using technology. These were some of Leyden's predictions:

- Networked personal computers, and their future successors in digital technologies, are every bit as revolutionary as the printing press—perhaps more so.

- The microprocessor at the heart of personal computers warrants comparisons with the motor that fostered the Industrial Age economy and society. But it's arguably bigger, even more powerful than that.

- Digital technologies are fundamentally new communications tools that greatly expand the power of the individual, who can now publish almost instantaneously to millions of people around the world for very little cost.

- Our educational system, our culture, even our institutions of government—all the things that define our public lives—are poised for some cathartic changes.

- Educators are just beginning to be aware of these new tools and to fundamentally change their methods of teaching. Eventually, computer skills will reach beyond the upper tiers of society and across generations. All schools will teach the basic literacy of our times: computer literacy.

- As for our culture, digital technologies have the potential to tie together not thousands of isolated minds, as did the printing press, but billions. We don't think of ourselves as isolated now, but we really are, compared with the levels of connectivity that we soon will experience. It won't be long before people across the planet will be able to communicate instantaneously and have access to almost all the world's information and knowledge.

- The vast majority of today's computers have yet to be hooked up to the existing network. And our society is just embarking on the first stages of building an information infrastructure that will provide the foundation for the Digital Age.

- Once that's all in place, once we've spread basic computer literacy and once we've raised a generation steeped in these new technologies, then the real fun will start. That's when we'll see the real breakthroughs in creative thinking, the explosion of new inventions, new art forms. A second Renaissance.

- Someday, in the distant future, perhaps a couple of hundred years from now, people will look back and classify our 1994 with another era's 1450. They'll look back at the decades around the end of the millennium, those years surrounding the year 2000, and marvel at the changes that took place.

The message that came through loud and clear is that rapidly changing technology was happening and there would be incredible breakthroughs in the next 15 years. As we all know, his projections became true. At the time they were published, they had a profound impact on me and contributed to my interest in and involvement with technology and change. Now, if that 15-year corridor between 1995 and 2010 seemed fast, the pace is escalating even faster as time goes on. Imagine what will be commonplace 15 years from now! It boggles the mind.

If you ask young people why they use technology, most will not say, "I love technology." Technology is simply the means by which they are able to learn, connect, play, and laugh. They are plugged in and staying current on what's going on around them—but not so for many of the adults I know. When I read Leyden's articles back in 1994, I remember thinking that the marketplace would be very tough on those who were resistant to technology and change. I have come to realize that this is indeed the case. I have seen the ramifications of this resistance play out many times.

If you genuinely intend to take control of your own future, I suggest that you stop saying, "Technology and these tools are not for me" and start saying, "I am going to learn." Become fluid with technology so you can continue to learn, connect, and remain relevant—and, in many cases, remain employed. Confidence and competence in technology is becoming much more of a requirement than an option. Do yourself a favor. Find a friend or two who utilize some aspect of technology and social tools. Buy them a coffee and be curious. Ask them why they like the specific tools they use. What is the value? Which tools do they use, and how do they use them? How do they make it work? How does it fit into their busy lifestyles? Choose one social tool and be curious about it. Follow people who are successful and interesting. Listen in, and at some point you'll find a way to contribute, too. Figure out which tools best enable you to gather information on your greatest interests and strengths. Seek new information constantly while you respond to life's road signs. This modus operandi will aid you in your quest to reach your desired destinations.

Social media has become a fabulous tool for those interested in learning, connecting with like-minded professionals, identifying strategic opportunities, and gaining access to the right information at the right time. I have actively engaged in social media myself in the last year or so, and it's hard to put into words how much easier it is to learn and connect. In the past when we made connections with people, typically in person or on the phone, we did so without knowing if the connection would be a good one or worthwhile for both parties. Now, if people follow each other on social and professional networking platforms, they can quickly gain a sense of alignment or not, and when they reach out to have conversations, they have a much clearer sense of whether the collaboration will be a productive one.

By the way, collaboration, linking arms with others, is critically important today and will continue to be so in the future. It will make you or break you, connecting you with current and future opportunities. There are millions of people on social networks, and they're not going away. New social networks will come, and some of the existing ones will yield to new tools. You don't need to use them all, but please make a point to understand them and choose to work with those that suit your needs. Hanging around with people who say "Bah! Humbug!" to technology and social media isn't helping. Please know that it takes a fair bit of curiosity and observation to recognize the merits of social tools.

Follow Your Intuition

Deciding to follow your internal compass and figure out what will make the best use of your skills and interests often takes intentional exploration involving self-reflection, numerous conversations, and soul searching. Sometimes people just feel this sense of quiet discontent that they can't put a finger on. Knowing what you are passionate about is a critical first step. The strengths assessments discussed in Chapter 3 are powerful guides. And sometimes, being courageous enough to ignore other people and societal pressures and pursue your passions is even more important. I have worked with many clients who have pursued careers because of family and societal pressures. It is important for you and your family to rise above this noise and figure out what truly brings you joy. Everyone will be far better off as a result. The following story is a good example of the positive outcomes that can be realized when innate talents are finally discovered.

For the television show *Life to the Max*, I interviewed nationally recognized artist Jeffrey Hurinenko. Jeff was one of those kids tagged for medical school early on. He was bright, and he was strong in math and science—a winning combination, it seemed. Upon completing his undergraduate degree, he went to take the entrance exam for medical school. He sat down for the exam, but it just didn't seem right. He walked away, feeling sure that something else was out there for which he was passionate. The answer did not come easily or quickly, but Jeff remained committed to figuring it out. Over the next several years, he tried different business ventures, traveled to far-off lands, and engaged in countless conversations and interviews. Finally, he was introduced to an Italian artist. Jeff describes the moment as an epiphany. He knew it immediately. It turned out that painting is his passion, and he was more than willing to gather the necessary practice to produce the amazing art he does today.

Not playing to personal strengths is more widespread than many people think. The Gallup organization estimates that a mere 20% of the workforce is actually playing to their strengths regularly. I have advised people at all stages of their lives who feel unchallenged or unsettled or uncertain to put time and effort into identifying the things that they are really interested in.

Engage in Many Conversations

Whether you're just starting out in your career or you're already in the marketplace, talk to as many people as you can as you explore your interests. Passionate people cast a bright light, and there is much to learn from them. In fact, you may need to reinvent yourself deep into your career. The following story offers one way to get the ball rolling.

I was working with Mark at Wells Fargo. He was doing work that he was kind of interested in, but he definitely was not passionate about it, and he wanted that to change. Mark was committed to finding a new opportunity and redirecting his career. In the conversation I asked him, "Who do you know who is very passionate about what they do and very good at the work as well?" Mark named two people. I said, "Great! Now, what I want you to do between now and the next time we speak, which is a month from now, is have conversations with 30 people who are passionate about what they do and are very good at it." Mark said, "Thirty people? You've got to be kidding me. I just told you I know two." I said, "That's great. When you are talking with those two, ask them, 'Who in addition to yourself do you know who are very passionate about what they do and also very good at what they do?' And when they give you names, write them down, get their phone numbers, and contact them. Just keep asking everyone you speak with, 'Who else do you know?' Assure them that you'll be respectful of their time and ask them to inform the people they refer you to that you will be contacting them."

Together we came up with three questions for the conversations: What are you passionate about? How did you determine what you are passionate about? What keeps you going?

The day before our conversation one month later, Mark forwarded a spreadsheet listing 30 names and an overview of the discussions. When we discussed the experience, I asked him for his key learning. Mark said he learned something from every discussion, but only two of them really resonated with him. Twenty-eight of the conversations did not, and this was a key learning for him. As it turned out, the two individuals whose journeys and passions he most resonated with offered to mentor him, and they met several times with Mark. He was gaining clarity about his next move. Mark learned the value of true exploration and of having as many conversations as possible.

I have shared this story hundreds of times because I am amazed how many people put *so* much weight on a couple of conversations and then make life-changing decisions as a result. Here is an example: Mary, a mother of four, returns to school to study interior design. She is very successful with her classes and projects and is raring to go after graduation. She sets her sights on designing restaurants. In her first interview, the designer tells Mary that restaurant design is very gratifying but requires at least 90 hours a week. Feeling dejected, Mary walks away from her dreams because she is not willing to sacrifice her family.

Who says this interviewer is the industry authority? There are workaholics in virtually every walk of life. Designing restaurants may universally demand long hours, but I would venture to guess there are folks out there who have created opportunities with more reasonable hours and demands. Instead of giving up after one discouraging conversation, Mary could have taken some notes, thanked the interviewer, and proceeded to arrange meetings with many others in the industry to gain a clearer outlook on the positions and requirements in the field. Then she would be able to make an informed decision that would be beneficial for both herself and her family.

Once you've created a list of things you are really passionate about or that interest you, narrow it down to two or three. Then start talking to people. Those who regularly chat with passionate people gain incredible insight into their own passions. When you finally match your passions or interests with your strengths, you will have a winning combination. I have talked with many people who think that identification of employees' greatest talents and strengths is their boss's job. The number one job of the boss is to get the job done. Your job is to determine your strengths and how to leverage them to create value for yourself and the organization in which you serve.

Regardless of whether you're working inside or outside a company, there will be key people in your life who will help you as you endeavor to figure out what you're best suited to do. There also will be people who disagree with the exercise and will try to discourage you.

Utilize Supporters

I believe there are three different types of supporters: "Been There, Done That," "Walk a Mile in Another's Shoes," and "I'll Always Love You, but That Doesn't Mean I Won't Challenge Your Assumptions."

There is great value in "Been There, Done That" supporters, who often are referred to as mentors. These folks may be in your industry, but they may be outside your industry as well. Fresh perspectives and creative innovation can come from these relationships. Be sure to ask them early on to challenge your assumptions and provide honest feedback in all interactions. There is also great psychic value for the "Been There, Done That" folks working with bright and ambitious protégés. Ask them to give you a run for your money and make their time and yours well spent.

The "Walk a Mile in Another's Shoes" supporters are the people who are on a similar journey as you. Having partners on a similar journey provides key learning. They also provide needed support and, from time to time, a shoulder to cry on or an empathetic heart to listen to you unload your frustrations. My business partner, Greg Stiever, and my friend Lisa Jansa, CEO of Exsulin Corporation, have been this type of supporter to me. The benefits of my relationships with them have been immeasurable.

Conversations with people who are in different businesses can be highly beneficial as well. While it is common to gravitate toward those with similar businesses, there is much to learn from those in different businesses. Their insights can be just the thing to give you fresh ideas and break up a logjam. The best questions I have learned to ask, regardless of the business, are:

- Tell me your story. Tell me the good, the bad, and the ugly about your journey.
- What has worked? What has not worked?
- What are your biggest lessons learned?
- If you had a chance to do it over again, what would you change? What would you do the same?

The third supporter is "I'll Always Love You, but That Doesn't Mean I Won't Challenge Your Assumptions." (If you think of a shorter name for this one, let me know—*wink!*) These supporters are friends who know you well and are familiar with your desires. They may not know all the details, but they have a general idea of the big picture you're shooting for. They'll love you even if you get off track, and they'll gently let you know. They'll also challenge your assumptions and try to help you stay on the path to a well-rounded you. They are advocates for your journey.

Utilize Doubters

There inevitably will be doubters along the way. The doubters are quick to tell you that they don't think you can do it, whatever "it" may be. For some people, the drive to prove them wrong is a huge motivator. If doubters turn on your inner motivation, go ahead and listen to them, and then get inspired to take action.

I have long been guided by focusing on what I want, but doubters have played a positive role in my accomplishments over time. Example one: When I got my first job, I decided to ride my bike to and from work. It wasn't a long ride by today's biking standards, but it was seven miles each way. Couple that with the fact that I was riding a pitiful 10-speed bike with a wheel that was uneven and made a jerking movement every rotation. I told my brother of my goal and later overheard him telling the family that he doubted I would do it. Six hundred and fifty miles later it was obvious that his doubts had kept me going. Example two: When I was a senior in high school, I was a narrator and actor in a church musical. After the performance, a woman who was a family friend approached me and said, "Laura, I had no idea you had any talent whatsoever." Her words have no doubt served me in a positive way. I never felt vengeful, just motivated.

For other people, doubters have a huge demotivating impact. If doubters bring you down, learn to deflect them. They're easy to spot because they constantly use words like *can't, don't,* and *won't.* To put it into *Seeing Red Cars* terms, the natural tendency when people hear negative comments is to stop the car, put it in park, and sit with those comments, thinking about them. It takes intentional discipline to recognize that the source of the comments is a doubter and you need to deflect the doubter, shift your car back into drive, and *keep on going* toward what you want.

The most important factor here is awareness. Being aware of the difference between supporters and doubters and how each affects you positively or negatively will enable you to identify these forces and to keep reading the road signs effectively as you go along in your journey.

Deal Effectively with Weaknesses

We all have strengths and weaknesses. At my company, On Impact, we definitely play to our strengths, and we are very good at finding folks with strengths in the areas in which we are weak. We have linked arms with some very talented people, and the products and services we bring to the marketplace are much better as a result.

Once you have a clear picture of your strengths and weaknesses, perhaps after completing a strengths assessment like those discussed in Chapter 3, make a point to really acknowledge and own your weaknesses. Awareness of your weaknesses enables you to work on neutralizing them or bring in folks who have strengths in the areas where you are weak. Recognize that this can be very hard to do because for many of us, the natural tendency is to hide our own weaknesses. We've been doing it all our lives. We may be so good at hiding our weaknesses that we actually have a hard time pinpointing them ourselves. But it's very important and well worth your time to flush out your weaknesses so you can address them. If you need help to do this, be courageous enough to ask for honest feedback.

My client Maria was experiencing challenges in her leadership role and decided to seek help to identify the problems. Maria is a brilliant scientist who had built an impressive career path that eventually led to leadership. She did a masterful job of playing to her own strengths, but she lacked ability to help others play to their strengths. She is extremely task-oriented and had a tendency to take on everything herself. Her division was under a lot of pressure, and she realized she could not do everything herself, but she had difficulty delegating and communicating with her team. As a result, progress had stalled.

Early on, we were talking about collaboration, delegation, and growing and developing her team. When I mentioned that what had gotten her to her new position (i.e., her personal scientific accomplishments) was unlikely to make her successful going forward as a leader and manager, this stark reality was an unwelcome realization. It sent Maria into self-protection mode. She defensively made a comment about not needing to collaborate with her employees because she's smarter than they are.

That statement gave me pause and led me to believe there was an unacknowledged weakness lingering under the surface. Her comment was the kind of natural, emotional reaction we can all make when we feel threatened. Inside, Maria's subconscious was saying, "What I'm hearing is outside my comfort zone." So she defensively responded with a statement intended to deflect a concept that was uncomfortable to her.

I remained curious and kept asking questions. It soon became apparent that she was scared witless of being a leader and relinquishing control. She was, however, very driven to success and was willing to shore up this potentially deal-breaking weakness. Maria truly wanted to succeed in her leadership role.

It was a long and arduous journey. We had to dissect the process and break it into bite-size pieces. She had to learn step-by-step and repeatedly practice how to identify the strengths of her employees, how to leverage those strengths to accomplish team goals, and how to interact with her employees in all types of situations. These were new behaviors for her. She slowly had to develop trust and confidence in letting go and competence in her leadership role. Letting go can be particularly challenging for folks who have a track record of flying colors. Like Billy McLaughlin, she was really bad and awkward at the leadership role for a long time. She continued to use her passions and strengths, but the new role required her to significantly improve her management weaknesses. She eventually overcame her resistance by being willing to listen to outside feedback. When people stick with it, making these improvements brings them great pride. Maria was no different. She's the first to admit she will never be awarded Miss Congeniality, but she is grateful that she worked hard to develop her ability to align the interests, strengths, and values of her employees to the right opportunities and to delegate appropriately, and she has a loyal and hardworking team to show for her efforts.

Once we know our strengths and can articulate them both verbally and in writing, and we acknowledge our weaknesses and learn how to address or compensate for them, we will be able to position ourselves better for projects, customers, opportunities, and jobs well suited to our greatest personal assets.

Take Charge in the Business World

Operating with the *Seeing Red Cars* mind-set while constantly seeking information and responding to life's road signs applies to teams and organizations as well as to individuals. When they all do this, great things happen.

In today's rapidly changing world, success will rely more on people, teams, and organizations operating with intention and taking charge of their own destinies—steering toward opportunities that leverage their greatest strengths and away from those that do not, all the while responding to life's road signs (e.g., the economy, technological advancements, generational differences, and diversity).

Futurist Jim Carroll says, "Clearly the rate of change—whether with business models, product life cycles, skills and knowledge—is speeding up. With such change, there is a lot of uncertainty within many industries as to what to do next." The reality is that product life cycles are collapsing. Products introduced today may last 6 to 12 months, whereas only a few years ago product life cycles were several years or more. Whole industries, organizations, and professions will change, rise, and be eliminated in a decade or less.

The need for leaders to steer their organizations' future is growing in importance. A blog post by Anne Pershel, founder and president of Germane Consulting in Worcester, Massachusetts, addresses this reality: "Good leaders see when patterns are ABOUT to change. While everyone else is looking at a clear bright picture of the present the savvy leader sees the vague outline of an emerging pattern through the incoming fog." That is how good leaders are operating when they use a *Seeing Red Cars* mind-set to develop an acute awareness of the marketplace. They anticipate change, and they lead innovations. Dr. Pershel suggests ways for people to practice the art of seeing into the future:

- Look for data (not just numbers) over a broad and varied horizon. Look in unusual places.

- Observe, study, and understand universal motivators and patterns of behavior.

- Note fleeting thoughts and hunches that typically fly into your mind almost without notice and then escape quickly without your attention. Later, when the hunch emerges as a reality, you will recall the fleeting thought.

Today and into the future, the constant pressure to innovate means dramatic changes in the way individuals and teams operate. We will all use technology much more as a tool to enable collaboration, connections, and commerce. Individuals, teams, and organizations will succeed when they consciously align people's greatest strengths and interests with the tasks that need to be completed, engage with others inside and outside the organization through the wonders of technology, and stay connected with new developments and trends in their industries and the marketplace.

The organization of the future must be change-adaptive. Simply identifying what we want without a keen awareness of our challenging and rapidly changing times could prove disastrous for individuals and for organizations. Individuals must knowingly gather the right skills and insights to remain relevant and valuable as the world changes. This is the only way that individuals, teams, and organizations will succeed, as industries, products, services, and professions come and go at breakneck speed.

One great example of a way that companies can drive their own futures and respond proactively to increased technology and marketplace changes is the Results-Only Work Environment (ROWE).

In the early 2000s, leaders at Best Buy Corporation, the technology retailer, decided to listen to an innovative idea proposed by two employees, Cali Ressler and Jody Thompson. The women recognized the potential for greater productivity when everyone is allowed to control when, where, and how they work. As long as employees meet their objectives, according to their ideas, the way they spend their time is entirely up to them. The ROWE concept is that everyone benefits when the focus is changed from hours to outcomes.

The company agreed to test the concept, and the results were noticed immediately. Gradually, it spread to all 4,000 of Best Buy's staff at its Minnesota headquarters. The women went on to share the success story through their book, *Why Work Sucks and How to Fix It*.

According to the authors, productivity is up an average of 41% on ROWE teams at Best Buy and other companies where ROWE has been implemented. Employees and managers alike seem to love ROWE, and voluntary turnover at ROWE companies decreased by up to 90%. Corporate America, take note: Concepts like ROWE are proactive responses to the conscious effort to scan the marketplace and create innovative systems to conduct business in ways that leverage people's strengths and interests. Innovations like this are the wave of the future.

We all want to remain relevant, employable, and ready to capitalize on opportunities for innovation. We want to operate with a frame of mind that does not allow fear to intervene and block our efforts. I suggest that you start *Seeing Red Cars*, steering toward opportunities, steering away from hazards, and taking positive actions toward what you want.

CHAPTER 5

Craft Personal "I Wants"

*I*n this chapter, you will start building your own plan. The sooner you identify your "I want" statements and write them down, the faster you will chart a meaningful course toward your desires. In a rapidly changing world, it's easy to lose sight of the big picture, which is why I am such a stickler for clearly defining what you want in all aspects of your life.

We are all at our best when we are striving for something. Clearly defining what you want, both personally and professionally, provides a guidepost as well as a target to keep you intentionally in the driver's seat and charting your own course. Problems can arise when we are on cruise control. People ask me how to create a change-adaptive culture, and I always say it's not so much about being change-adaptive as it is about people and teams being engaged, awake, and striving for personal and professional improvement. Resistance will always be present in the workplace, but it is much less evident in an engaged culture.

Striving for a Well-Rounded You

The discussion in this chapter is broadened to focusing on what you want in a more well-rounded way, because if one area of your life is out of whack, it's likely that others are feeling the pinch as well. The goal is to constantly strive for balance. I've seen a good number of folks who are really making strides toward what they want professionally and somehow lose sight of the big picture and what they want in the other areas of their lives. I believe this is especially true during times of dynamic change, when there is a good bit of uncertainty. Welcome to our world. In this chapter, you will begin the process of forming coherent "I want" statements that will lead to a more well-rounded you.

Awareness of Values

The line between our personal and professional lives is blurring. Now more than ever before, it's important to be acutely aware of our passions, interests, strengths, *and values*. Values are those things you hold dear or esteem highly. Carefully consider your values when it comes to both you and your job.

Years ago, I was working with Gerald, a manager who was interviewing a candidate for a new position. As fate would have it, I knew the candidate, Tina. Knowing what I knew about the department and the position, I knew it couldn't have been a worse fit for Tina. It was a very thorough and calm culture, and Tina was a fireball! She loved the *idea* of the job. She was reacting to the job title rather than matching her strengths and personal values with the responsibilities of the position. In reality, the culture was a misfit for her. Tina's list of values may have included words such as *excitement* and *activity*, whereas the company valued such things as thoughtfulness and structure. Nonetheless, Gerald said the company was committed to simmering her down, and Tina said she was committed to instilling much-needed energy into the lackluster department. I feared that both Tina and the company would experience major frustrations as the company pressured her to conform. Tina happened to be pursuing multiple opportunities at the same time, and at my urging, she engaged in some deep introspection about her strengths and values. She ended up matching her strengths and values with a position at another company. In the next role, she was a golden girl, and the work and organizational culture were a good fit. She later told me that each of the positions she subsequently held was immeasurably gratifying, to boot.

RED CARS Toolkit

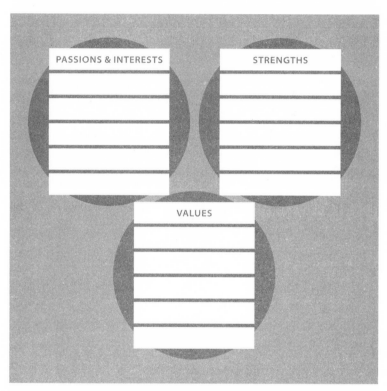

PASSIONS & INTERESTS

STRENGTHS

VALUES

Tool 2 Add values to your worksheet from Chapter 3

Clarifying your values is important at this point because you must take into account your fundamental personal values as you determine your "I want" statements later in this chapter. Open your Red Cars Toolkit PDF and select Tool 2. You'll notice the

Values column is at the bottom and your first two completed columns, Passions & Interests and Strengths, are at the top. Now, think about what you truly value. Here is a list of sample values to get you started:

Abundance	Achievement	Adventure	Appreciation
Boldness	Bravery	Challenge	Execution
Courage	Creativity	Curiosity	Agility
Flexibility	Decisiveness	Determination	Giving
Integrity	Outcomes	Autonomy	Mastery

There are hundreds of values from which to choose. Pick five values that truly resonate with you, and enter them in the third column on this worksheet.

Now it's time to put together your own personal plan. Four activities from the Red Cars Toolkit will guide you step-by-step through the process. Working with individuals at all levels within organizations, I have used these tools for more than a dozen years. They will help you flesh out your personal desires (i.e., your Red Cars "I want" statements) in light of your passions and interests, strengths, and values and the environment in which we live. All of these factors must be taken into account to uncover your true desires, prioritize them, and drill down to the top three to five "I wants" that will make the greatest difference for you within the specific time frame you set for yourself.

Please, don't just gloss over these steps. I have had numerous clients who insist they "know" themselves, but when they genuinely take time to work through this process, they discover certain aspects of their lives they have been ignoring or overlooking for years that turn out to be deeply important to them in light of their personal values.

RED CARS Toolkit

BUCKET LIST
for a well-rounded me

What I want...

☐ _____

☐ _____

☐ _____

☐ _____

☐ _____

☐ _____

☐ _____

☐ _____

☐ _____

☐ _____

☐ _____

☐ _____

☐ _____

☐ _____

Tool 3 Brainstorm everything you want

Start with the personal *Seeing Red Cars* Bucket List (Tool 3). This exercise will help you reconnect with all the things you have thought about or said that you want in your life. Use it to brainstorm a free-flowing list of everything you want. Think about yourself, your family, and your long-term goals. Think about categories like money, health and fitness, family and friends, spirituality and faith, volunteer work, and travel. Start gathering all of your thoughts.

If you find yourself running out of ideas, look at these categories to remind yourself of things you have said you want in your life:

Career	Personal growth education
Money investments	Fun recreation travel
Money income	Physical environment home
Health and fitness	Spirituality faith
Friends and family	Volunteer work
Romance (Significant other)	Other

This exercise can make a profound impact on you. I once led a session in which I asked the participants to brainstorm about anything they have ever said or thought that they would want in their lives. A friend of mine was in the audience. When I next visited his family's home, I noticed his list of "I want" statements was posted for all to see. When I read his list, one statement stood out above all the others: "I want to give at least a million (dollars)." Wow. There were no fancy cars or dream homes or the typical luxury items listed. There were statements like "I want to put my kids through college" and "I want to take care of my mom as she ages." It made me stop and think: If he is able to give at least $1 million, isn't it highly likely that he and his family will reap many personal gifts along the way? It was such a poignant way of expressing an "I want" statement. It also illustrates one additional attribute: Don't create self-imposed stopping points on your achievements. Using the phrase "at least" opens you up for not only meeting but also exceeding a particular goal.

RED CARS Toolkit

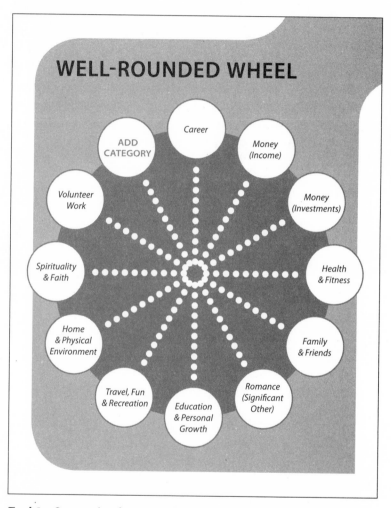

WELL-ROUNDED WHEEL

Career

Money (Income)

ADD CATEGORY

Money (Investments)

Volunteer Work

Health & Fitness

Spirituality & Faith

Home & Physical Environment

Family & Friends

Travel, Fun & Recreation

Romance (Significant Other)

Education & Personal Growth

Tool 4   On a scale of 1 to 10, where are you now with your goals?

The *Seeing Red Cars* Well-Rounded Wheel serves as a snapshot of your perception of where you are now with your personal "I wants." The center of the wheel is your starting point (0) following the spokes out to each life goal (10). Darken the circle where you think you are at this time, on a scale of 1 to 10, in achieving what you want in each category. Using the Well-Rounded Wheel of the Red Cars Toolkit, you can click the circle to mark your dots. Now, if you were to connect the dots from spoke to spoke, how bumpy or smooth would your ride be today? The more well-rounded your life, the more smoothly your wheel will turn.

RED CARS Toolkit

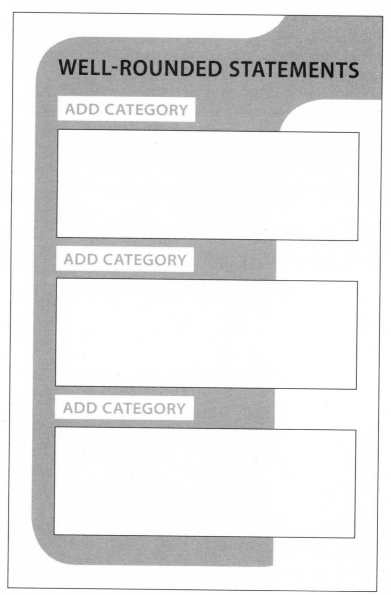

WELL-ROUNDED STATEMENTS

ADD CATEGORY

ADD CATEGORY

ADD CATEGORY

Tool 5 Where do you want to be?

Page 8–11 of the Toolkit is where you clearly define what you want by writing *Seeing Red Cars* Well-Rounded "I Want" Statements for all 11 categories (plus a few more, if you desire) from the personal wheel. This is the place for collecting, organizing, and prioritizing what you want. Generate several ideas for each category (select the categories from the drop-down menus, the gray rectangles, and then type your "I want" statements in the boxes). Eventually, you will prioritize and choose your favorites. Joe's sample worksheet in Chapter 3 may give you some ideas. Be sure to write at least one statement in all 11 categories, plus any that you have added.

Here are the categories for reference:

Career	Education/Personal growth
Money investments	Travel, fun and recreation
Money income	Home/Environment
Health and fitness	Spirituality and faith
Family and friends	Volunteer work
Romance (Significant other)	Other

If you're thinking, "Huh? I'm not sure how to do that," here are some guidelines that I've developed through working with hundreds of people. These will help you get the job done more expeditiously.

Clarity is the most important motivator and predictor of future success. In fact, the biggest reason people procrastinate and fail to get off the mark is a lack of clarity. When "I want" statements are vague, shaping actions around them is nearly impossible.

Next, make sure that your "I want" statements are *positive and affirming*. Since people have a natural tendency to focus on what they don't want and are preprogrammed to avoid problems, it's very easy to verbalize an "I want" statement that is negative in nature. People say, "You're right, I need to focus now on what I want," and then in the next breath say, "What I want is to not have crabby people in my life." Because they used the word *want*, they improperly perceive that they are "focusing on what they want." A better statement of this objective is "I want positive people in my life." Make sure you're asking someone to check your "I want" statements so that they are positive and affirming. Otherwise, we're back where we started.

Make sure that your "I want" statements are *specific, measurable,* and have a *timeline.* If you can assign numbers and specificity to your goals, they will motivate you to take action. For example, you may say, "I want to read more." But if you don't declare your intention in a way that is specific, measurable, and has a timeline, chances are you will make only a slight improvement. Instead, specify "I want to read one book a week," "I want to read 20 pages a day," or "I want to read three chapters a week." That gives you something to rally around, and it releases the energy, creativity, and motivation to take the necessary action.

The more specific and measurable your "I wants," the easier it is to take action and track your progress. Assigning a specific timeline and target completion will really get you going. I've seen people add a timeline to an "I want" statement, and suddenly the plan, people, and needed circumstances begin to "magically" fall into place.

So as you write your "I want" statements, focus on *clarity,* being very *specific,* identifying what you *want,* making it *measurable,* and creating a *timeline.* It's amazing how creative and ambitious people get when all these aspects are in play. They truly become accountable to themselves. It really works.

Coming up in Chapter 7, you will build your own *Seeing Red Cars* Action Traction plan by breaking down your "I wants" into daily, weekly, and monthly actions. Caution: It's important to not overwhelm yourself, or you may discard all of your "I want" statements and slide back into status quo. The Action Traction plan will help you narrow your lists of "I want" statements and prioritize the top four or five. You'll start building your action plan around the first or second priorities, to start. Once you start experiencing successes, your energy and enthusiasm will grow, and you can add other goals along the way.

Balance the Important Aspects of Your Life

When you're writing your "I want" statements, the best approach is to combine passion, strengths, and values with marketplace confidence and competence. Now you have a winning combination. It is entirely worth the time and effort to do this because whenever there is a marked difference between personal you and professional you, it is likely to be stressful, and I'm willing to bet that neither your personal life nor your work life is getting the best of you. The following story of Craig is an example of a well-intentioned leader who truly lost sight of the big picture when work demands overshadowed the other important aspects of his life.

Craig was leading a major division of a retail organization that was trailing the others in his company. The ever-mounting pressure began to affect Craig's relationships with his team members. The harder he tried, the worse things became. Craig was a born-and-bred achiever, and the faltering results were getting the best of him. A history of being an A student, a Division I football player, and the recipient of a very early promotion in his job had led Craig to believe that hard work equals results, always. Hard work is critical, but rest and rejuvenation and connecting with loved ones can contribute to success in important ways. In this case, his anxiousness and angst were showing, and team members were intimidated by his size, his stern facial expressions, and his commanding presence.

In reality, Craig is a compassionate and truly empathetic leader, but his inherent strengths were getting lost under the pressure.

The lack of sleep and exercise wasn't helping either. In our conversation, we began talking about what brought him joy and a sense of lightness, as opposed to the burden he was bearing. The subject of his three kids under the age of seven came up. I asked him to tell me a cute kid's story about one of his children. I anticipated that his demeanor and his outlook would shift to create a place for us to talk about how differently he felt when he was talking about his children, the value of those cherished moments, and the sense of perspective they bring. Craig pondered the question. "A cute kid's story, hmm," he said. Finally, he indicated that a story just wasn't coming to mind, and we moved on.

At the end of the conversation, I asked Craig what the most important takeaway from our session was. He became very quiet. He said, "You must have realized it, back at the point when you asked me to tell you a cute kid's story. It wasn't that I couldn't come up with one, it was that I didn't *have* one. You see, I start work at 4:30 or 5 in the morning. I'm not home before 10, ever. Often, I don't get home until midnight. I don't get to see my kids much. I work weekends. I'm working tirelessly to make the necessary improvements. I've had the sense that I'll make things better and then reconnect with my family. Now it occurs to me that they are the answer here."

Craig suddenly realized that the way he was living his life was inconsistent with what he truly wanted long-term. His lack of family time and the opportunity to rest and rejuvenate was actually getting in the way of turning the division around. It was a defining moment for him. He made the decision at that moment to put effort into a more balanced lifestyle. He began working more traditional hours and spending more time with his family. His attitude and work behavior improved, and he found that he was making better decisions and utilizing his staff more effectively. Counterintuitively, working less and increasing his family time helped him accomplish more and better results at work.

Seeing Red Cars Means Driving with Intention

In the past few chapters, we started out by identifying your passions, interests, and strengths. Next, we mapped those against the marketplace, technology, skills, and awareness needed to remain connected and relevant. That order was not by accident. Without this insight, people identify "I want" statements that have more to do with their neighbor's, spouse's, or parents' expectations or with a single conversation or article they read than with their personal strengths, passions, and values, along with a comprehensive scan of marketplace trends. They say to themselves, "It looks like the marketplace is going there, so I'll go there." Oops! I want to emphasize that the goal should be to blend your strengths with a proven direction the marketplace is going, and it is highly unlikely that you will gain a full understanding of where you fit best from a single conversation or article. Talk to many people to gather a well-rounded perspective.

The *Seeing Red Cars* mind-set allows you to use the best that you have at your disposal to define your life and career and make sure that you remain relevant, well connected, and proud of where you end up.

The first time I wrote "I want" statements by using this process was in 1995. I identified a one-year timeline. The categories I chose were career, money-income, money-investment, health and fitness, friends and family, spirituality and faith, and volunteer work. In the career category, my statement was "I want to start a business and identify a partner to work collaboratively with by Dec. 31." Initially, I wasn't clear about either the type of business or the partner I was seeking. Setting the timeline got me to start talking with people—lots of people—in my network of contacts. That helped me develop a clear picture in my mind of the business and led me to meeting a great business partner who shared my vision.

I was able to accomplish six of my "I want" statements within 11 months. One of them was a little bigger leap, and it took a little longer, but I was able to accomplish that one, too. With the one-year timeline, I saw the fruits of this exercise quickly. It made me a believer. I will caution you to make sure that all of your "I want" statements are aligned with and complementary to your passions, interests, strengths, and values. The more you incorporate these factors into your statements, the more powerful they will be to you. It will also increase the likelihood that you will accomplish goals with longer-term effects rather than short-term fixes. Author Daniel Pink cautions that short-term goals can lead to short-sighted outcomes. So do this: Focus on your passions, strengths, and values, and choose an appropriate timeline for you. Write it down. Most important of all, *do it!*

Before you complete the bridge worksheet (Tool 6) that follows, I want to provide context for its importance. Think about Peter Senge's tension illustration described earlier, from *The Fifth Discipline*. The left box on the bridge worksheet, WHERE I/WE ARE, represents the pole on the left side of Senge's illustration, and the right box, WHAT I/WE WANT, represents the hand on the right side. You are in the middle with rubber bands around your waist. Senge states that the juxtaposition of the left side, representing where you are, relative to the right side, representing what you want, "causes natural creative tension, and the natural tendency of tension is to seek resolution." If you focus on "I don't wants," you are subconsciously pulled toward the left. If you intentionally focus on "I wants," you are pulled toward the right. Learning how to generate and sustain creative tension so you are pulled toward the right gives you a powerful tool toward achieving what you want.

In the bridge tool that follows, you will take it one step further and drill down to your top priorities in the coming year, your "must haves," and your priorities that are "nice, but not necessary."

This part of the exercise also leverages the Pareto principle (aka the 80/20 rule), which states that roughly 80% of the effects come from 20% of the causes. Translated to business, 20% of your efforts will yield 80% of the results, so determine which 20% of your "I wants" listed under "must haves" will produce the greatest value for you. This will give you clear priorities around which you can build a plan to drive purposely toward your "must haves" and achieve what you *do* want. Remember, you get more of *whatever* you focus on.

RED CARS Toolkit

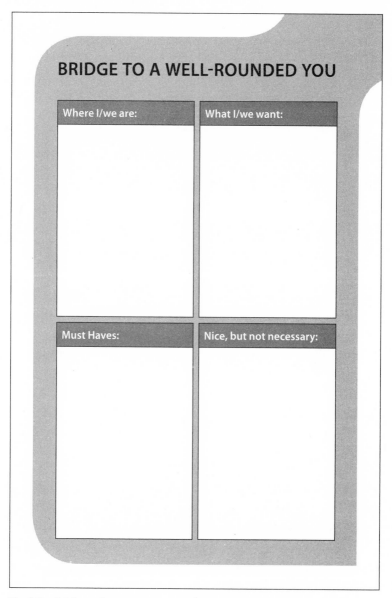

BRIDGE TO A WELL-ROUNDED YOU

Where I/we are:	What I/we want:
Must Haves:	Nice, but not necessary:

Tool 6   Bridge where you are to where you want to be

Here's where you bring all of the activities together. Scroll to the personal Bridge worksheet on page 12 in the Red Cars Toolkit PDF. It might help to review Joe's sample bridge worksheet as you complete this exercise.

1. First, under WHAT I/WE WANT in the upper right corner, choose five categories from the personal wheel (Tool 4) and enter one category per space, along with your favorite "I want" statement from that category, on the well-rounded statements worksheet.

2. Second, under WHERE I/WE ARE in the upper left corner, type a statement that describes where you are right now with each of your top five "I wants."

3. Third, under MUST HAVES in the lower left corner, choose the two or three most important "I wants" (from the upper right), and enter them as "I want" statements with a defined timeline (1 year? 3 years? 5 years?).

4. Finally, under NICE, BUT NOT NECESSARY, enter the remaining two or three "I want" statements.

This bridge exercise allows you to see everything in one place and visualize the lay of the land. In Chapter 7, you will refer to this worksheet as you create your Action Traction plan, plotting monthly, weekly, and daily actions to begin driving toward your most important "I wants."

Be Mindful of External Factors

Up to this point, I've been addressing factors that primarily are within your control: the personal identification of your passions, strengths, interests, and values and how to write your personal "I want" statements and chart a course toward your desires. All of these activities are useful, but the real world can interject lots of factors that may interrupt your progress or completely redirect your course.

I'd like to touch on two external factors to be mindful of as you go about working on your "I wants": seasons in life and patterns of behavior. Constant, conscientious awareness of these factors helps you avoid slipping back into behavior that is not in alignment with your long-term goals.

Seasons in Life

I always tell people that there are seasons in life. Seasons have a beginning and an end. They are part of life. They are unavoidable.

Seasons in life may come about when you are called on to care for the needs of children or aging parents. When you have babies, you are going to go without adequate sleep for a while, plain and simple. It's unavoidable. It's times like this when life can get out of whack. Our balance, our priorities, and what we want from a more holistic standpoint can really get off track.

There are also times when it is easier and important to go back to school, to travel more, or to log the necessary hours to get an important project or business off the ground. When these seasons arise and our needs change, we have to find ways to adapt our schedules.

I remember my own journey down the changing-needs path. When my children were young, I was desperate for a flexible schedule or a decreased client load for a few years. I was an award-winning sales rep with a solid reputation, but neither the company I worked for nor the countless companies I talked to would even *consider* a flexible schedule. I chose to start my own business and have never regretted the move.

Sometimes the seasons are born of unwanted circumstances. They can be times of real imbalance in our lives. For instance, when my dad was dying, there was no balance in my life. I wasn't sleeping or eating correctly. In fact, I remember thinking that both were overrated. Exercise? Yeah, right. Community involvement? Are you kidding me? I felt fortunate to have matching socks and to manage taking care of the basic needs of my family. This is one of many seasons in life. As I mentioned, they have a beginning and an end, and we all recognize they are part of life.

At times, it can be very hard for people to recognize or accept that a season is over. There are reactionary and creative responses to life's circumstances, or what I call life's seasons. I first advise people to acknowledge that what they are going through is a season that will eventually end. Once they are ready to be creative, they will begin crafting solutions to deal effectively with the situation, to learn from it, to move on, or to find its silver lining. When I'm working with people who are experiencing life-changing circumstances, or seasons, I ask them, "How long will you react to this change in your life? At what point will you move from being reactionary to being creative?" I advise them to "put a stake in the ground" and assign an ending date. They may choose a timeline that is either too short or too long, but at least they are making a conscious decision rather than allowing their unconscious reaction to linger a lot longer than the season warrants, which can end up being far more damaging.

Patterns of Behavior

Then there are patterns of behavior to watch out for. When behaviors become patterns that are not consistent with what we want long-term, they can be problematic. The earlier story of Craig, who was working at the expense of his family time, is a good example. Without the guideposts and specific targets of our "I want" statements, we run the risk of developing a pattern of behavior that could block our ability to achieve success in a well-rounded way. Being clear about what you want will allow you to remain on track. If you are unsure whether a pattern of behavior is getting in your way, look again at your well-rounded wheel. Are there categories you ranked low in terms of where you are currently? Go to your trusted advisors and ask for help: "Will you help me figure out if there is a pattern of behavior that is preventing me from achieving what I want in this area of my life?" If a pattern is identified, acknowledge it, call it out, and add it to your Action Traction plan.

The answer, once again: Actively engage the *Seeing Red Cars* positive outcomes mind-set while driving intentionally with high beams on. You retain control.

Chart Your Professional Plan Next

The next chapter provides a parallel set of activities to map your professional "I want" statements in the same manner as we charted your personal "I wants" in this chapter. I will close with a story to show that it's never too late to complete the Red Cars Toolkit exercises and completely change your life.

Years ago, I worked with a law firm in transition. They were opening new offices and changing the functions of an existing office. A senior partner, Walter, who had worked at the firm for more than 40 years, had recently retired and was struggling with too much free time. Work had consumed him his entire life, and he had been divorced more than two decades earlier. He was still involved with the firm's strategic direction but not the day-to-day functions. Walter decided to join us for our Monday morning muffin meetings.

There was much conversation regarding the practice, their strategy, and their plans for growth and recruitment. All staff members went through the process of writing personal and professional "I want" statements. The notion of personal "I want" statements was foreign to Walter, but strangely attractive at the same time.

At the next meeting, Walter arrived holding his personal "I want" statements, and he was eager to share them with the group. His statements included:

- I want to spend quality time with my family and friends twice a week. (Initiating activities was new to him.)
- I want to exercise for one hour five days a week. (All work and no play had left him with numerous ailments.)
- I want to travel for at least a week twice a year. (Too much work had caused him to forgo vacations.)
- I want to get a designer to redesign the first floor of my home within the next two weeks. (His house was painfully outdated and screamed bachelor workaholic.)
- I want to complete the redecoration of the first floor of my home within the next 90 days.
- I want to get involved in one committee with my church. (He had attended church but not given back to his church community because of his demanding workload.)
- I want to meet someone I can spend time with and enjoy, and they enjoy my company, too. (He had not dated since his divorce.)

Since Walter spent more time at home than at the office, here are the types of Red Cars triggers that could help keep his "I wants" at the top of his mind (see the "Triggers" section at the back of the book for a full list of ideas):

- A picture or painting of a red car on a wall
- A scale model of a red car displayed in a central location in his home
- Post-it Notes with "I want" statements near his phone, on his nightstand, or on his bathroom mirror
- Red accessories in his car
- A red-painted door (e.g., garage service door)

I worked with Walter one-on-one for several months. He

took the monthly, weekly, and daily actions associated with his personal "I want" statements very seriously. After six months, I began receiving notes and calls of gratitude from his family and friends. His daughter still works at the firm. Walter's story proves that being successful both personally and professionally leads to a more balanced life that cannot be achieved with success in a career alone. It's never too late.

Now, before you drive on and get clear about your career "I wants," please take a break. You've done a lot of work so far. Let the first set of worksheets process in your mind. In Chapter 6, you'll complete Red Cars exercises to become well-rounded in your professional life, too.

Craft Professional "I Wants"

What is most important to you in your professional or work life? In this chapter, you will take the "I want" exercises one step further and complete the same set of activities with the focus on clarifying your greatest "I wants" in the development of a well-rounded "professional you."

There is an important caution for you in this chapter: When it comes to your professional or work life, social conditioning and past experiences create *powerful subconscious expectations* in people who are not *purposefully* aware of their influence. As we said in Chapter 1, unless people devote conscious effort to focusing on what they want, an estimated 70% of their thoughts are subconsciously focused on what they don't want or what they are trying to avoid. These negative thoughts can act like the ocean's undercurrent, suddenly grabbing you and tugging you under the surface if you aren't paying close attention.

We talked about social conditioning and past experiences in Chapter 1, and it's worth refreshing our memories at this point. Our families are the first place that social conditioning begins, and then it continues with our schools and includes the people we hang around with, the work we do, and the environment with which we surround ourselves.

I remember a conversation with a client in which he recognized that he had developed an expectation for positive peer relationships and poor leader relationships in his work life. His dad and uncles had always complained about their bosses, but they had enjoyed their relationships with coworkers. This social conditioning had caused him to focus on what he didn't want with leaders and what he *did* want with peers. Reflecting back, he realized that these unconscious expectations had set him up for challenging leader relationships since he had started working. It didn't matter who the leaders were. He approached situations with an unconscious internal list of "I don't wants" that had clouded his relationships with those in leadership roles.

To combat this tendency, my client could write a statement such as this: "I am aware of my leader's priorities, and I make sure to address them first so that our interactions are productive and positive." Approaching his leaders with this preprogrammed intention in his mind would set him up for effective interactions. The same goes for you. Defining what you want in your work relationships is the way to tap into your stored positive expectations and overcome the natural tendency for your actions to be influenced by unconscious negative social conditioning. Remember, you get more of *whatever* you focus on.

Sample of Seeing Red Cars Professional Worksheets

Before you complete your own professional "I want" worksheets, again, it will be useful to see a completed example. For this example, Lily is a financial services sales expert who has been working for 10 years. She completed the following Red Cars activities:

- Passions & Interests, Strengths, and Values (*Tool 7*)
- Professional Bucket List (*Tool 8*)
- Professional Well-Rounded Wheel (*Tool 9*)

- Professional Well-Rounded "I Want" Statements (*Tool 10*)
- Professional Bridge Worksheet (*Tool 11*)
- Action Traction 52-Week Plan

Review Lily's example before you begin.

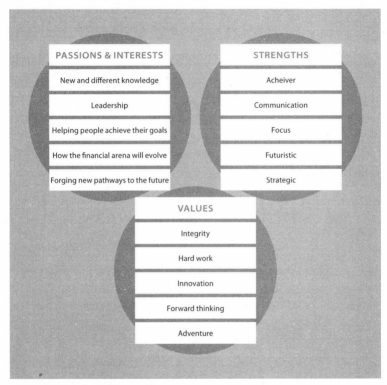

PASSIONS & INTERESTS	STRENGTHS
New and different knowledge	Acheiver
Leadership	Communication
Helping people achieve their goals	Focus
How the financial arena will evolve	Futuristic
Forging new pathways to the future	Strategic

VALUES
Integrity
Hard work
Innovation
Forward thinking
Adventure

Tool 7 Lily's Passions & Interests, Strengths, and Values

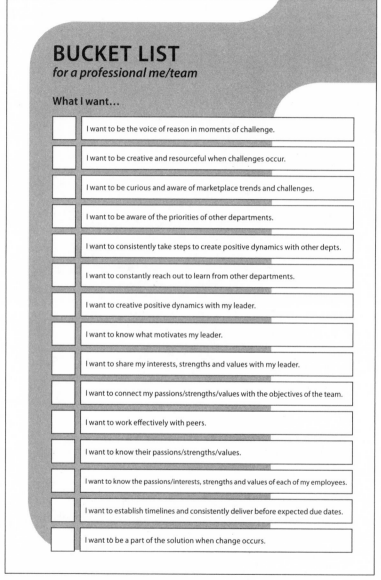

BUCKET LIST
for a professional me/team

What I want...

- ☐ I want to be the voice of reason in moments of challenge.
- ☐ I want to be creative and resourceful when challenges occur.
- ☐ I want to be curious and aware of marketplace trends and challenges.
- ☐ I want to be aware of the priorities of other departments.
- ☐ I want to consistently take steps to create positive dynamics with other depts.
- ☐ I want to constantly reach out to learn from other departments.
- ☐ I want to creative positive dynamics with my leader.
- ☐ I want to know what motivates my leader.
- ☐ I want to share my interests, strengths and values with my leader.
- ☐ I want to connect my passions/strengths/values with the objectives of the team.
- ☐ I want to work effectively with peers.
- ☐ I want to know their passions/strengths/values.
- ☐ I want to know the passions/interests, strengths and values of each of my employees.
- ☐ I want to establish timelines and consistently deliver before expected due dates.
- ☐ I want to be a part of the solution when change occurs.

Tool 8   Lily's Professional Bucket List

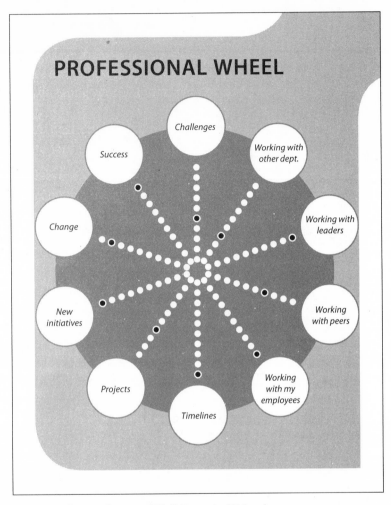

PROFESSIONAL WHEEL

Tool 9 Lily's Professional Well-Rounded Wheel
Note the position of the black dots. The center of the wheel is 0, and
the perimeter is 10.

PROFESSIONAL STATEMENTS

CHALLENGES

I want to consistently be resourceful when facing challenges.
I want to consistently be part of the solution as challenges are encountered.

WORKING WITH OTHER DEPARTMENTS

I want to consistently work corroboratively with other departments.

I want to consistently seek to learn about the strengths of other departments.

I want to consistently seek first to understand and then be understood in my communications with other departments.

I want to consistently be seen as a force for positive change and commitment to finding the best solution.

I want to consistently be seen as a get-the-job-done kind of professional

WORKING WITH LEADERS

I want to consistently seek the passions/interests, strengths and values of my leader.

I want to consistently make connections between my passions/interests, strengths and values and the objectives of the time.

I want to consistently seek to understand the best method of communication for my leader and deliver communication via that method.

Tool 10 Lily's Professional Well-Rounded "I Want" Statements

BRIDGE TO A PROFESSIONAL YOU

Where I/we are:

I want to work effectively with other departments.

I am more loyal to my team and less so to other departments.

I tend to criticize, complain and roll my eyes about new initiatives.

I tend to get stuck with change.

I tend to second guess my ability to be successful.

What I/we want:

I want to use my Focus strength to meet our 1st qtr sales goals (Challenge)

I want to learn another department's best practice by May (w/other depts)

I want to offer ideas about the new project to my boss by 3rd qtr (New initiatives)

I want to find contacts who know about the website change by 2nd qtr and be part of solutions to improve our dept (Change)

I want to find a project outside my dept. that makes better use of my Communication skills by year-end (Success)

Must Haves:

I want to offer ideas about the new project to my boss by 3rd qtr (New initiatives)

I want to find contacts who know about the website change by 2nd qtr and be part of solutions to improve our dept (Change)

Nice, but not necessary:

I want to use my Focus strength to meet our 1st qtr sales goals (Challenge)

I want to learn another department's best practice by May (w/other depts)

I want to find a project outside my dept. that makes better use of my Communication skills by year-end (Success)

Tool 11   Lily's Professional Bridge Worksheet

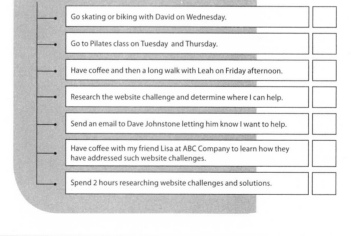

ACTION TRACTION

Personal Must Haves:

- I want to schedule and plan special time with my family and friends each week.

- I want to schedule one-on-one activities with my son every week.

- I want to get together with friends at least once a month and have coffee with a girlfriend twice a month (Family and Friends).

- I want to get physically healthy by exercising for 45 minutes three times per week (Health and Fitness).

Professional Must Haves:

- I want to offer ideas about the new project to my boss by 3rd qtr (New initiatives)

- I want to find contacts who know about the website change by 2nd qtr and be part of solutions to improve our dept (Change)

Actions:

- Go skating or biking with David on Wednesday.

- Go to Pilates class on Tuesday and Thursday.

- Have coffee and then a long walk with Leah on Friday afternoon.

- Research the website challenge and determine where I can help.

- Send an email to Dave Johnstone letting him know I want to help.

- Have coffee with my friend Lisa at ABC Company to learn how they have addressed such website challenges.

- Spend 2 hours researching website challenges and solutions.

Tool 12 Lily's Action Traction 52-Week Plan (Week 1)

With Tool 10, you will create professional "I want" statements in the 10 categories on the *Seeing Red Cars* Professional Wheel: *challenges,* working with other *departments,* working with *leaders,* working with *peers,* working with my *employees,* establishing solid *timelines* and executing them, *projects, new initiatives, change,* and *success* so that your passions and strengths can shine. *This is one of the most important activities in this book.* Of the 10 categories on this wheel, the four categories on the right side, beginning with "Working with," concern your relationships with others and are easier to effect changes quickly. The remaining six categories relate to your expectations for your work life. These require longer time frames and harder work to produce changes.

Being crystal clear about professional "I wants" can absolutely make a marked difference for people or can be what trips them up and causes them to miss out on the opportunities that would play to their greatest talents and strengths. Even being unclear in two or three of these categories can allow subconscious "I don't wants" to take over and influence your thoughts and actions. If you don't consciously resist, the natural tendency to focus on what you don't want creeps in and gets in the way of what you want to accomplish professionally. And you can be totally unaware that your past experiences are creating your current reality!

Again, awareness is key. Without awareness, past experiences and subconscious social conditioning win. With awareness and purposefully written "I want" statements in each of the categories on the professional wheel, you retain control of life's steering wheel, and you are much better prepared to consciously navigate through the potentially negative undercurrent of past experiences and social conditioning.

Clarifying Professional "I Wants" Leads to Autonomy

In Daniel Pink's book *Drive,* he states that "one of the things we are driven by is autonomy." Autonomy is the capacity of the rational individual to make an informed and uncoerced decision. It's fundamental to our happiness. Pink says, "We all long to be autonomous and to have control over our lives and destiny." It just makes sense, doesn't it? We all know people who do not have autonomy in their line of work who seek control elsewhere. When you don't have autonomy, you are more likely to resist such things as change or direction from your leaders. During those times when you lack a sense of control, you are more likely to slip back into fear and concern and focus on your "I don't wants." Fight that tendency by maintaining intentional focus on your "I wants." Again, you get more of whatever you focus on. If you're thinking about red cars, you'll see them everywhere.

In reality, no matter what stage you are in your work life—just starting out, mid-career, or a later stage—you will do yourself and your family a favor by clarifying your strengths, interests, and values as they relate to both your personal and *professional* life and by defining what you want in all 10 *Seeing Red Cars* Professional Wheel categories. When you find a career opportunity that truly plays to your strengths and interests and is aligned with your personal and professional "I wants," you will win, and your organization will win, too.

Finding professional alignment is a lot like dating, actually. When you consider the person you are likely to marry, you intuitively consider your fundamental values compared with those of your potential spouse or significant other. Do they match? Are they polar opposites? You are not likely to change the individual you choose to marry or the company you choose to join. Making the right marriage and career decisions are critically important for your success and satisfaction.

At this point, you may be thinking, "So how do I go about achieving alignment so that I can make better decisions?" The exercises you are about to complete will show you how.

So let's get clear about your professional wants by guiding you through the following six *Seeing Red Cars* professional "I want" activities. Note: Each of these activities can be completed on your own and with your work team using the same *Seeing Red Cars* professional worksheets (i.e., what "I want" when working by myself or with my work team, and what "we want" as a team).

RED CARS Toolkit

Tool 7   Add to your Passions/Interests, Strengths, and Values

Go to page 13 in the *Seeing Red Cars* Toolkit PDF. Think about your professional or work life and reread the lists of words you entered on this worksheet. Do additional words come to mind that further clarify what's important to you, from a work perspective, in each of these categories? If so, add those words to this worksheet. If nothing more comes to mind, that's okay. The most important action was to review the list and refresh your memory before moving on to the next exercises.

RED CARS Toolkit

BUCKET LIST
for a professional me/team

What I want...

☐ _____

☐ _____

☐ _____

☐ _____

☐ _____

☐ _____

☐ _____

☐ _____

☐ _____

☐ _____

☐ _____

☐ _____

☐ _____

☐ _____

☐ _____

Tool 8   Brainstorm Your Professional Wants

In the Professional Bucket List, enter everything you have thought about or said that you want in your professional or work life. Think about the 10 Professional Wheel categories and consider: Do I prefer to work independently or with others? Do I prefer structure? Do I like managing others? Does change excite me, or do I avoid it? Do aggressive timelines invigorate me or make me feel anxious?

If you find yourself running out of ideas, look at these categories to remind yourself of things you have said you want in your professional life:

Leaders	New initiatives
Peers	Change
My employees	Success
Timelines	Challenges
Projects	Other

RED CARS Toolkit

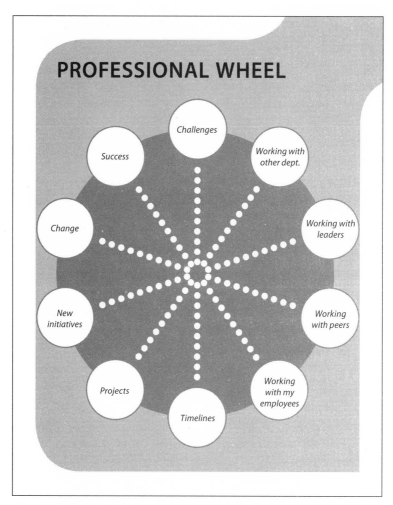

PROFESSIONAL WHEEL

Challenges

Success

Working with other dept.

Change

Working with leaders

New initiatives

Working with peers

Projects

Working with my employees

Timelines

Tool 9 On a scale of 1 to 10, where are you now with your professional goals?

Just like the Personal Wheel, the center of the wheel is your starting point (0) following the spokes out to each career goal (10). Darken the circle (or click on the editable PDF on page 17) where you think you are at this time, on a scale of 1 to 10, in achieving what you want in each category.

RED CARS Toolkit

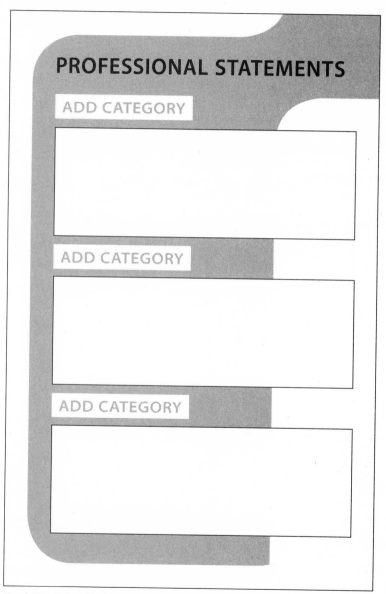

Tool 10 What Do You Want Professionally?

Go to page 18 in the Toolkit PDF. Pick the four or five categories from the professional wheel that are most important to you in the coming year. You will narrow down to one Professional "I Want" Statement for each category you choose. Enter the goals in the gray boxes, and start drafting "I want" professional statements that apply to each goal. Remember to use the five criteria for writing "I want" statements: focus on clarity, be very specific, identify what you want, make it measurable, and create a timeline.

Here are the Professional Wheel categories for reference:

Success	Timelines
Challenges	Projects
Working w/other departments	New initiatives
Working with leaders	Change
Working with peers	(add your own here)
Working with my employees	

RED CARS Toolkit

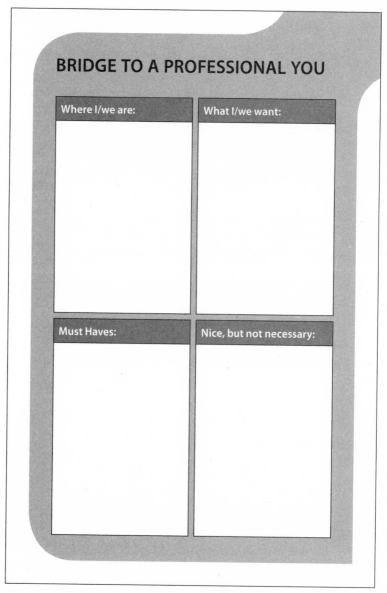

Tool 11   Professional Seeing Red Cars Bridge

Now you will combine your top priorities in one place. Scroll to the Professional Bridge Worksheet (Tool 11) on page 22 in the Red Cars Toolkit PDF. It might help to review Lily's sample bridge worksheet in Chapter 6 in this book.

1. First, under WHAT I/WE WANT in the upper right corner, choose five categories from the professional wheel (page 17) and enter one category per space, along with your favorite "I want" statement from that category on the well-rounded professional statements worksheet (starting on page 18).

2. Second, under WHERE I/WE ARE in the upper left corner, type a statement that describes where you are right now with each of your top five "I wants."

3. Third, under MUST HAVES in the lower left corner, choose the two or three most important "I wants" (from the upper right), and enter them as "I want" statements with a defined timeline (1 year? 3 years? 5 years?).

4. Finally, under NICE, BUT NOT NECESSARY, enter the remaining two or three "I want" statements.

You should now be far better prepared to evaluate any job opportunity or career decision you face. Use the information you gathered through this process to remain focused on your greatest assets and desires.

Your Environment Influences You

If your family has a history of complaining about work experiences, companies, and jobs, it is likely that you, and subsequently your children, will behave in the same manner. If social conditioning has led you to believe it's inevitable that the company you work for will take advantage of you, you will probably end up in such an organization and perpetuate the process by lamenting about the injustices of the working world. Later on, your children, having observed you doing this for years, will be set up for a similar journey.

Conversely, if parents have found their work to be rewarding and gratifying, their children are likely to create for themselves an equally gratifying work experience.

If you land in a work environment that diverges from what you want and makes you feel stuck because of what you have come to expect from social conditioning, get out of it fast. There *are* miserable leaders, teams, and organizations, but no one is forcing you to stick with them, other than you and your expectations.

Position Yourself Better by Focusing on Professional "I Wants"

Very few of the recent college graduates I have worked with evaluate their first work experiences favorably. Tragically, it often doesn't get better with subsequent positions. A friend of mine who is a recruiter told me a story about a young professional (Carlos) in pursuit of his second job. Carlos had accepted his first job with high expectations and had been profoundly disappointed. He was determined to avoid all of the ills of the first position. When Carlos was contacted by an organization for an interview, he prepared by creating a list of what he didn't want in the position:

- I don't want a team that crumbles at the first sign of significant change.
- I don't want an organization that is siloed or departments that are uncooperative.
- I don't want bad leaders.
- I don't want peers who don't hold themselves accountable.
- I don't want soft timelines.
- I don't want projects that are low on the totem pole of the company's priorities.

- I don't want a culture that is change-averse and resistant to new initiatives.

Carlos was proud of his list, and once he got going, he developed quite the momentum in explaining the list. He thought that sharing this list with the interviewer would communicate what he actually *did want* and that the interviewer would understand that Carlos's intention was to deliver the opposite of these statements. The interviewer did not grant Carlos a second interview, even though he was well-suited for the job. The recruiter later found out it was because of the negative impression left by Carlos's "I don't want" list.

The recruiter told me he now helps candidates prepare for interviews by discussing with them what they *want*, along with the attributes they will bring to the company to help it achieve its goals. So how could Carlos have approached the interview differently? I'll contrast each of Carlos's statements with its positive version:

What Carlos Said He Didn't Want	What Carlos Wanted
A team that crumbles at the sign of significant challenge.	A team that welcomes challenge and collaborates to come up with strategy and effective solutions.
An organization that is siloed or departments that are uncooperative.	A work culture that rewards collaboration and access to departments, where sharing leads to better solutions and innovation.
Bad leaders.	Great leaders dedicated to growth and the development of each of their employees.
Peers who don't hold themselves accountable.	Peers who hold themselves responsible to projects and outcomes and own up to mistakes that are made along the way.
Soft timelines.	A culture that supports timelines and executing them.
Projects that are low on the totem pole of the company's priorities.	Projects that are valued and have top organizational priority.
A culture that is change-averse and resistant to new initiatives.	A company that is change-adaptive and committed to creating new successful projects and then taking action to move toward them.

If Carlos had stated his desires in this way, he may actually have been hired by that company and could still be there today. Being clear about what you want will get you going in the right direction for the right projects, organizations, teams, and leaders. If there is a mismatch, be grateful to learn it early on. When you have an "I don't want" list, people can't help you make connections with the right projects. I believe that your ability to clearly identify your passions, interests, strengths, and values, along with what you want, and to articulate how your attributes will benefit the right project, team, or organization will bring your best self to the projects at hand and increase your chances for alignment. People who tend to be selected to work on the best projects get very good at matching themselves with the right organizations, the right projects, and the best team members. Remember, you get more of whatever you focus on.

Dig Deeper Than the Job Title

I always advise people to not get hung up on job titles. I was working with Molly, and we had gone through the process of identifying her passions, strengths, and values and developing her personal and professional "I want" statements. Molly was in the process of searching for a new job. Through the Red Cars professional "I want" exercises, Molly clarified that she:

- is passionate about working with people and is very good at it
- has strong written and verbal communication skills
- enjoys working with a company's most valued clients and bringing new clients into the business
- enjoys building leadership skills in younger team members
- enjoys communicating with the media

Molly came to me with an "ideal position" she wanted, and she asked me to help her prepare for the interviews. The position title was managing partner, which at this company is equivalent to CEO or general manager. So I asked Molly, "Tell me about the position and the specific responsibilities of the position." It turned out that Molly was unclear about the specifics. The managing partner title is what had caught her eye. Through our conversation, she made the decision to talk with the person who currently held the position and find out what the responsibilities would be and, most important, what percentage of time she would spend on each.

Molly came back with a list and we laid it down next to her professional "I want" statements. It was a telling moment. Molly found out that the position was highly analytical. It had more to do with strategic direction than dealing with people. It involved no creative writing and no customer contact unless there was a problem. She would have very little interaction with the professional development of others. Only 5% to 10% of the time would be spent doing the activities that would really lean on her passions, strengths, and values. She recognized that indeed this was not her "perfect job."

The likelihood of your being able to find a position that is aligned with your "I wants" is significantly greater if you're really clear about your passions, interests, strengths, and values; you gather the skills necessary to remain relevant and connected; and you clearly identify what you want professionally.

The Red Cars Mind-Set Is Equally Important in Daily Interactions

Success in your professional life has a great deal to do with your thoughts and behavior in day-to-day meetings and interactions. Too often this is overlooked. Your professional "I wants" should guide you, like a compass or GPS, backed by intentional daily actions with all the personalities and situations you encounter.

I was seated on a flight next to a leader who had seen the *Seeing Red Cars* film at a corporate event at which I spoke. He acknowledged the importance of focusing on what you want, and with the goals and objectives of the organization, but he felt that his thoughts were not apparent to others and inconsequential to his overall success.

I shared with him this story: I once received a call from a highly frustrated client. She was coleading a project, and her counterpart was making her crazy. After listening to her explain the dynamics of the project and their relationship, it was apparent that she was a get-the-job-done type of gal, and her colleague was a do-the-job-right type of guy. It was also apparent that she did not appreciate a single thing that he brought to the project. Not one! I asked her, "What is his sense of the project and your feelings about him?" To this she said, "He has no idea." In reality, I am confident that he did indeed have a very clear sense of her feelings, and he wasn't enjoying the process any more than she was.

Unless you are an Emmy Award–winning actor, it is likely that your thoughts, too, are obvious to others. Whether you realize it or not, people have a pretty good sense of what you are thinking, and it affects your meetings, interactions, and relationships. Being intentional about what you want in these settings, especially with those people you find the most challenging to work with, creates more productive outcomes almost immediately.

Keep Individual and Team Wants Top of Mind

The rate of change in our world is accelerating, and with rapid change comes greater volatility. Knowing your passions, strengths, and values is critical. Mapping them against marketplace skills, trends, and the competencies needed is an absolute must.

Students entering college today will graduate into a world that holds opportunities that don't currently exist. At any given moment, a new innovation could all but eliminate the need for your company, product, project, or profession. For the people, teams, and organizations that are paying attention, there is tremendous potential for new opportunities. There are signs all around us of innovations, and if we are dialed in to these trends and changes, we can gather the skills needed to create new opportunities as they arise. Being clear about what you want in your professional life will put you in a better position to take advantage of these opportunities.

I mentioned earlier that the set of Red Car exercises in this chapter can also be completed by your work team to gain clarity on what "we want" as a team. Your work team can either do the exercises proactively to set the stage for positive work interactions or pause and complete the exercises to help redirect team members if they have gotten off track. The latter scenario can be very challenging but ultimately is always worthwhile.

I once worked with an organization that placed a high value on client interactions (i.e., "The client always comes first"). On the surface, this sounds like an honorable cause. In practice, this focus gave every employee a perfect excuse for being late for meetings. Upon arriving late, a quick excuse that the delay was caused by a client need relieved the pressure on that person in the moment. This client-focused intention, while great for clients, led to much frustration. The norm for meetings was to start 10 minutes late. The norm for behavior was beginning a meeting and explaining things once again each time stragglers arrived. This lack of respect for meeting timelines migrated to project timeliness, and expected completion dates were a joke. Team dynamics were stressed, and team members felt less important than clients. It was a problem that had grown out of control. Water cooler conversations focused on frustration, lack of productivity, and the belief that most excuses about "client needs" were unfounded and just plain excuses. Something had to change.

The problem was so pervasive that senior management addressed the situation head-on. The company developed a "we want" statement with regard to meetings that became one of its five strategic priorities for the coming year: "We want to consistently respect timelines for clients as well as for each other (meetings, projects, objectives)." It was a significant culture change, and it took a great deal of intentional effort with everyone reminding each other when actions veered off track. Ultimately, the changed behavior created dramatic improvements in all aspects of running the business and successfully completing projects.

Work teams can avoid this deterioration of coworker respect by proactively creating "we want" statements to guide group relationships. There is tremendous value in work teams clearly defining what "we want" for our projects and within our organizations. Teams that do this realize extraordinary outcomes. So use these exercises to get clear about your own personal and team wants, and then work with your work team to define "we wants." You will start realizing a more positive work culture and dramatic improvements in your career.

You might be feeling a little overloaded right now. You've done a lot of work. Congratulations. The next step is to create your Action Traction plan, so take another break. When you're rested and refueled, we'll resume our journey.

CHAPTER 7

Turn Actions into Outcomes

You've done a lot of work so far to get crystal clear about your personal and professional "I wants" and to write them all down. It is now time to plot a deliberate course of action. Those of you who love planning and to-do lists are saying, "Cool! Let's get started!" But what about those of you who *hate* task lists and prefer to operate in hottest-priority-at-this-moment mode? This chapter serves both ends of the spectrum.

In Chapter 1, we introduced scientific evidence of how the brain works and how we can reprogram our brains to focus on what we want. In this chapter, we discuss a second phase of brain science that is equally important to understand: Success in changing deeply ingrained habits and achieving our "I wants" requires time, effort, discipline, and physically planning, tracking, and checking off action steps daily, weekly, and monthly. As I mentioned earlier, on the *Seeing Red Cars* professional wheel, the four "Working with" categories on the right side refer to the relationships in your work life. When you act on your "I wants" in these categories, you can start to see results quickly. The remaining categories on the wheel represent deeply ingrained behaviors. The notion of changing these behaviors in 21 to 30 days is unrealistic. From my perspective, it typically takes six months to a year or more.

Once we understand *how* the brain learns new information and *why* it takes intentional repetition, visualization, and action over days, weeks, and months, we can proceed to:

1. *Think it:* Control our thoughts.

2. *See it:* Visualize positive outcomes.

3. *Do it:* Take deliberate monthly, weekly, and daily actions.

We will also discuss in this chapter the importance of evaluating your progress and making necessary adjustments along the way, how feedback from the right people greatly aids your efforts, and how helping others achieve what they want promotes progress toward achieving your own goals.

Control Your Thoughts

In Chapter 1, we introduced the concept of neuroplasticity—the brain's natural ability to form new connections. Our brains use the outside world to shape and reshape themselves as new information is introduced. We overcome bad habits by adding intentional new approaches such as focusing on what we want and aligning our thoughts, actions, and behaviors toward desired outcomes. It's like creating a new neuron pathway, or road, and then choosing to act on the desired changes. Our brains restructure to facilitate the process.

The formation of new brain pathways is only part of the benefit of the *Seeing Red Cars* mind-set. Repeated, intentional behaviors provide significant psychological benefits. An article by Nick Tasler in *Business Week* cites experiments done by psychologists Shelly Taylor at UCLA and Peter Gollwitz at New York University. They found that when people think about implementing a decision they have already made (such as their personal and professional "I wants"), it puts them in a far better mood. As you may recall from Chapter 1, creating new roadways in the brain triggers the central nervous system to produce chemical reactions and release serotonin, which lends itself to creativity, innovation, and focus. According to Taylor and Gollwitz, a positive outcomes mind-set significantly raises our self-esteem and makes us feel more in control of the world around us. The researchers call this the "implementation mind-set," when we mentally shift gears to implementation.

Understanding the way the brain works is the first step in effectively turning action into outcomes. Once you have that foundational knowledge, you can proceed to create an Action Traction plan, track your progress, and *persevere.* You must *stick with it* until it becomes second nature. Using the Action Traction planner (Tool 12) and deliberately deciding on and tracking monthly, weekly, and daily actions will lead to the achievement of your "I wants." Neglecting this modus operandi is the one factor that can absolutely derail your efforts and prevent success.

Visualize Positive Outcomes

Additional research validates the power of visualization and the length of time it takes to achieve sustainable change. In *The Brain That Changes Itself,* Norman Doidge cites early brain research by Alvaro Pascual-Leone, a pioneer in brain research. While Pascual-Leone was a young medical fellow at the National Institute of Neurological Disorders and Stroke, he used transcranial magnetic stimulation (TMS) to conduct experiments that demonstrated how people learn skills and create sustained change. In one study, he analyzed the power of visualization. He taught two groups of people who had never studied piano a sequence of notes, showing them which fingers to move and letting them hear the notes as they were played. The members of one group, the "mental practice" group, sat in front of an electric keyboard, two hours a day, for five days, and imagined playing the sequence while listening to the notes as they were played. The second "physical practice" group actually played the music two hours a day for five days. The brains of both groups were mapped before the experiment, each day during the experiment, and afterward. Then both groups were asked to play the sequence, and a computer measured the accuracy of their performances. Pascual-Leone found that both groups had learned to play the sequence, and both showed similar brain map changes. Remarkably, mental practice alone produced the same physical changes in the motor systems as actually playing the piece. By the end of the fifth day, the changes in motor signals to the muscles were the same in both groups, and the imagining players were as accurate as the actual players were on their third day. When the "mental practice" group finished its mental training and was given a single two-hour physical practice session, its overall performance improved to the level of the physical practice group. The study proved that mental practice before physical practice is an effective way to prepare for learning a skill.

The actual practice of visualization is simple, and I advise my clients to do it regularly as they prepare for situations both large and small. Here's how: Close your eyes and picture yourself engaged and successful in doing what you want. It doesn't matter what the situation is. You may be preparing to be an effective speaker, a powerful parent, or a skillful project manager. What matters is that you can see with a great deal of clarity the outcomes you want.

In another study, Pascual-Leone mapped the brains of blind subjects learning to read Braille. The subjects studied Braille two hours a day in class and one hour a day at home, five days a week, for one year. These studies were among the first to confirm that when human beings learn a new skill, neuroplastic change occurs.

But one of his most surprising discoveries, with major implications for learning and change, involved the way that changes occur over time.

Subjects were mapped with TMS on Fridays, at the end of the week's training, and on Mondays, after they had rested for the weekend. Pascual-Leone found that the changes were different on Fridays and Mondays. From the beginning of the study, Friday brain maps showed rapid and dramatic expansion, but by Monday these maps returned to their baseline size. Friday maps continued to grow for six months, stubbornly returning to the baseline each Monday. Monday maps, however, showed an opposite pattern. They didn't begin to change until six months into the training. At that point, they increased slowly and then hit a plateau at 10 months. Although the changes on Mondays were never as dramatic as the Friday maps, they were more stable over time. At the end of 10 months, the students took 2 months off. When they returned, they were remapped, and their brain maps were unchanged from the last Monday mapping two months earlier. Thus daily training led to dramatic short-term changes during the week, but more permanent changes were seen on Mondays over time. Pascual-Leone believes that the differing results on Mondays and Fridays suggest differing plastic mechanisms. The fast Friday changes strengthen existing neuronal connections and unmask buried pathways. The slower, more permanent Monday changes (aka "the Monday effect") suggest the formation of brand-new structures, probably sprouting from new neuronal connections and synapses.

"The Monday effect" validates our belief that success in adopting the *Seeing Red Cars* mind-set to achieve desired outcomes requires time, effort, and discipline. Striving for our "I wants" takes intentional, repetitive actions to create and sustain change. If you sincerely want to work toward your goals, use the Action Traction

52-week plan (Tool 12) to enter the specific action steps and their completion. Those who are resistant to using planner systems, take note: You have to *want to* change, and you have to *intentionally* record your progress. It takes discipline and effort, but it is *highly* worthwhile.

Do It!

The final Red Cars tool, the Action Traction 52-week planner (Tool 12), is a separate PDF to download from www.seeingred-carsbook.com. Do that now.

RED CARS Toolkit

ACTION TRACTION

Personal Must Haves:

- [ ]
- [ ]
- [ ]

Professional Must Haves:

- [ ]
- [ ]
- [ ]

Actions:

- [ ]
- [ ]
- [ ]
- [ ]
- [ ]
- [ ]
- [ ]

Tool 12 Seeing Red Cars Action Traction 52-Week Plan

Your Action Traction 52-week plan (Tool 12) will bridge the gap between intention and action. Whenever you act on what you want to have happen, new pathways in your brain begin to develop. But you need to establish clear action steps to keep moving forward. It may help to refer to Lily's example in Chapter 6 as you start building your plan. Schedule a weekly time, perhaps every Friday, to update your plan for the following week. Include actions you intend to complete toward each of your top MUST HAVE "I wants." To get started on your first weekly plan, refer to the MUST HAVES on your personal bridge (Tool 6) and your professional bridge (Tool 11), and enter action steps in your Action Traction planner (Tool 12). Along with this weekly tool, enter daily actions and monthly goals in your day planner system or electronic calendar, such as the one in Microsoft Outlook. Using my reading goal as an example, enter "Read 20 pages a day" on your daily to-do list, "Read 3–5 chapters a week" in the Action Traction planner, and "Read 1–2 books a month" as a monthly goal in your calendar system. Add statements like these for each of your top personal and professional "I want" categories. Work your way through the list, and check off each action step when you've accomplished it. If it helps to refer regularly to your plan, you can print *Seeing Red Cars* Action Cards (www.seeingredcarsbook.com) on card stock, trim them, and write down your next few action steps to carry with you in your wallet or purse. Then, as you complete actions and achieve an "I want," pick another "I want" from your bridge tool and keep on tracking!

There is great psychic value in reviewing your actions regularly and taking stock in your progress. Practicing this discipline enables you to track how long it takes to accomplish a MUST HAVE and identify those actions that create the greatest value. Action Traction gives you the traction you need to accomplish what you want—one want at a time!

Some of the actions you enter may be stretch goals, so remember to take it slow. Enter step-by-step actions and discipline yourself to do at least one challenging task each day. Breaking down your top priorities into small steps makes it easier to discern which ones will involve outside coaching, training, mentoring, and other resources. When you focus your efforts in this way and take actions in the most impactful areas, you will realize meaningful change, and improvement will be obvious—not only to you but to others. You will be motivated to keep on going.

Planning Directs Your Internal Compass

Controlling your thoughts and using visualization are powerful tools, and the Action Traction system helps you preplan and track your actions. However, the realities of life can often confound our intentions. It is easier to spend our time doing what is urgent but not important if we haven't clearly defined what we want. Granted, emergencies occur, but if we're unclear about what we're trying to create, emergencies tend to become more prevalent and commonly get in the way.

Knowing and doing what is important rather than reacting to what is urgent is fundamental to your ultimate success. In *First Things First,* Stephen Covey states that there is a clear distinction between decisions guided by the internal compass of what you want long-term, both personally and professionally, and decisions guided by the clock of scheduling. Preprogramming your internal compass sets you on the course for intentional actions that are much harder to derail when urgent but not really important "emergencies" try to intervene.

I once worked with a leader in a manufacturing company who exemplified urgent but not important. Paul was constantly drawn into the dramatics of life. We talked about identifying where he wanted to go and taking action toward it monthly, weekly, and daily. Paul was resistant to the process because he always had "an emergency." I teased him that he had missed his calling as a firefighter because he was always putting out fires. Paul had not yet made the decision to plot his course and commit to sticking with it unless there was a *legitimate* reason for something to intervene. Being clear about what you want and taking steady action toward it on a monthly, weekly, and daily basis will keep you in the driver's seat, dictating your actions and creating more of the outcomes you want.

A final caveat with regard to planning that can truly propel you toward your goals:

- Never end a day without identifying what you want to accomplish the next day.

- Never finish a month without clearly defining what you want to do the next month.

- Never conclude a week without clearly defining what you hope to accomplish the next week.

- Never plan a meeting or conversation without clearly defining and visualizing what you want.

In situations large and small, it comes down to intention and actions. It takes discipline, but it really works.

Evaluate Your Progress and Ask for Feedback—Often!

As you move along in taking action, it is critical to assess the effectiveness of your actions and to have partners you can talk with about your progress. Feedback is perhaps the most powerful tool to move you along on the path toward what you want. Many people struggle with this or aren't sure how to ask for feedback, so I have some tips. Start with "I want to improve" or "I want to get better." Then say, "What is one thing I could do less of, more of, or differently to improve my performance?" If what you're doing is largely on track, these questions may be difficult to answer. Asking the question in this way prompts the person to give you at least one tangible answer rather than a gracious acknowledgment of a job well done. Most people will be able to come up with at least one response.

Now that you know this question, make it your mantra! Asking for feedback regularly from a variety of trusted sources is a powerful way to move you along on your path toward what you want, personally and professionally. If people are reluctant, ask them for one thing and smile. Remember to smile. When you pose the question in an open way, people will often give one thing. The feedback you get will keep you growing and build your strengths. Additionally, people who ask for feedback are confident, so go forth and behave confidently.

At times when trusted advisors are not available, you can ask yourself these questions: What are the lessons I've learned? What has worked? What hasn't? It's important to make only a couple of changes at a time. Trying to make a number of changes at once makes it difficult to discern which tactics are working and which are not.

Your supporters can be very helpful to you once again. Analyzing which efforts are producing the most important outcomes for you, your team, and the organization may not be immediately obvious. Your trusted advisors can often help you identify the distinction between impactful and busy. Make sure you're seeking feedback from people who have the right insight to help you. Many people make this mistake repeatedly—going to family members, colleagues, and leaders who do not have the right insight, credentials, experience, or personal success to provide valuable feedback. Instead, constantly be on the lookout for people who are successful and respected for the work they do. Those are the people to ask for advice and feedback.

Accelerate Your Progress—Help Others Get What They Want

Now that you are seeking feedback, how can you accelerate your progress? This may seem counterintuitive, but the best way to get where you want to go is by helping others accomplish what they want. You will get there faster. How could this be? The incredible story of the transformation of a low-performing city school district in Manassas Park, Virginia, illustrates this phenomenon.

Manassas Park is a small city public school district in Virginia that had been struggling for years with problems ranging from inadequate resources to deplorable facilities. Mismanagement and personnel turnover were rampant. But the district's problems began to turn around in 1995, when the Manassas Park School Board hired a new superintendent, Tom DeBolt.

The Little School System That Could describes Dr. DeBolt as "a self-professed visionary and optimist." Between 1995 and 2005, he led the district's transformation into a model small city school system with fully accredited schools, championship teams, acclaimed extracurricular programs, and award-winning school buildings. DeBolt recognized early on that he could not achieve significant changes alone. He lived and breathed the *Seeing Red Cars* philosophy, guiding and encouraging his staff every day to focus on what they want for themselves, their teams, their schools, and the district. He began conducting annual retreats for his leadership team in 2000, coaching his team in the development of individual, team, and organizational "I wants." These goals served as guiding principles they referred back to often throughout the year.

DeBolt began with a vision and had more and more people define their personal and professional "I wants." Starting with individuals and spreading to teams and the organization, people turned actions into outcomes. It took a long time, considering the significant barriers and opposition they faced, but DeBolt and his staff stuck with the plan determinedly. They developed a pattern of behavior that became sustainable by getting a large group of people driving toward what they want. This should be the overriding objective of *any* business leader—to build a successful culture that is sustainable whether you remain there or not.

The results of DeBolt's positive outcomes mind-set, actions, and persistence have been incredible. He inherited a collection of ramshackle schools, a budget that had not kept pace with enrollment growth or inflation, and a track record of academic and administrative problems. A decade later, every Manassas Park school had achieved state accreditation under the provisions of Virginia's tough educational accountability program, the school system had won architectural awards for its innovative school designs, Manassas Park teams had garnered league and even state championships, and salaries for teachers and school administrators had grown to be more competitive with Manassas Park's far more affluent neighbors.

DeBolt could not have achieved these successes on his own. A model leader, he championed the cause, maintained his positive attitude and focus on the goals, and inspired everyone around him to rise to the occasion. By helping others focus on what they want, he achieved what he wanted.

If Manassas Park, Virginia, city schools can achieve this turnaround, any organization can. Fundamentally, it's simple. Start *Seeing Red Cars!*

CHAPTER 8

Drive Red Cars to Critical Mass

*I*open this chapter with a bold pronouncement: It *is* possible for an organization of employees who are *Seeing Red Cars* to hit critical mass—the existence of sufficient momentum in which the *intentional focus on wants* becomes a self-sustaining culture and fuels further growth. And where positive-focused cultures like this are achieved, the new reality of driving with intention and high beams on becomes *equally as powerful* as the old cruise-control, just-do-my-job frame of mind. The new reality does not easily return to the passive and subconscious existence of what I don't want and am trying to avoid.

Up to this point in the *Seeing Red Cars* journey, we have created insight into the unconscious focus on what you don't want or are trying to avoid, and we discussed what it takes to turn this thinking around and instead focus intentionally on what you *do* want. It is now time to demonstrate how this transformation can take place. I want you to think about what it might mean to you, as an individual, if you were a member of an organization in which the majority of employees are actively engaged in the discipline of focusing on actions to achieve desired outcomes. If you were surrounded by colleagues engaged in these behaviors, how powerful would those forces be to you on a daily basis? I suspect it would be a lot easier for you to maintain a Red Cars positive outcomes mind-set and not fall back into negative-thinking ruts.

In this final chapter, the stories of the transformation of a major division of an advanced biomedical company—we'll call it REDTECH—under the guidance of its dynamic leader, Robert, will illustrate how this transformation can be achieved. For REDTECH, it took about three years—three long, challenging years. Some of this company's stories have already been introduced in earlier chapters:

- Carla, in Chapter 1, the fence-sitter who was unsure and a little uncomfortable at first when asked to thoughtfully consider her true passions, strengths, and values. An assembly-line worker at the time, she realized through the process that she really loves finance and numbers and that she wanted to move into the accounting department. When she gradually started talking about the idea with her colleagues and manager, they encouraged her and gave her the confidence to focus on her true interests and values. She returned to school, earned her accounting degree, and has flourished.

- Maria, in Chapter 4, the brilliant scientist who built an impressive career path that led to leadership. She was driven to success, but she was extremely task-oriented and had a tendency to take on everything herself. Leadership skills were new to her, and she had difficulty delegating and connecting with her team. Progress had stalled in her division. Maria had to learn step-by-step and repeatedly practice how to identify the strengths of her employees, leverage those strengths to accomplish team goals, and interact with her employees in all types of situations. These were new behaviors for her. Maria was willing to seek the coaching and assistance she needed to develop competence in her leadership role. Today, Maria has overcome her potential deal-breaking weaknesses and has a loyal and hardworking team to show for her efforts.

- George, in Chapter 1, who was the classic detractor. He grumbled about how it was ridiculous that focusing on outcomes could really have an impact on things and that being aware of the challenges and difficulties was far more important.

Remember, we didn't focus on George in the beginning. We didn't leave him out, but we didn't focus on him. We focused instead on the 20%, the ambassadors who enthusiastically agreed with the *Seeing Red Cars* philosophy, and the 50%, the fence-sitters who recognized the value of focusing on what you want but were cautious and not ready to commit.

Over the course of three years, the *Seeing Red Cars* thought process at REDTECH went from being cumbersome and uncomfortable in the beginning, like new things often are, to being very fluid and comfortable. People were marching not only to their personal and professional "I want" statements but also to the statements, vision, and values of the organization. REDTECH finally hit critical mass the day that George, who had been defiant for so long, was leading a tour of the manufacturing facility. His colleagues were stunned and proud to hear him say, "The way that we operate here—the things that compel us, that get us up every morning, that have us wanting to get better day after day—is that we are truly guided by our vision. Each of us has clearly defined not only the organization's vision, but what we wanted to accomplish personally, and we are taking daily, weekly, and monthly actions to move toward those goals."

When the critical mass of an organization is comprised of individuals who are aligned and engaged; playing to their passions, interests, strengths, and values; focusing on what they want, both personally and professionally; and achieving individual, team, and organizational goals, great things happen. That's when organizations start to see the impact of having a large number of people actively scanning the marketplace, focusing on solutions and innovations, having the ability to be change-adaptive, and responding with positive actions based on what they *can* control. Companies that are adamant about getting people to utilize their strengths will prevail.

Turning around the damaging natural tendency to focus on what we don't want and what we're trying to avoid will take serious work over a period of years. But those companies willing to put in the time and effort will enjoy the fruits of their labors.

Reaching Critical Mass with Seeing Red Cars

The remarkable transformation of REDTECH, which hit critical mass with *Seeing Red Cars*, owes much of its success to its visionary leader. Robert, who has now retired, was executive vice president of manufacturing and operations in the 1990s. Robert slowly infused into this company the mind-set of the famous cathedral story: Three stonemasons hard at work were asked in turn what they were doing. The first said, "I'm sanding down this block of marble." The second said, "I'm building a wall." The third said, with a broad smile and a gleam in his eye, "I am building a cathedral."

Earlier in its history, REDTECH was in the midst of a crisis. Its primary product was used to bore out corrosion from industrial pipes. While the company's technology was highly respected, the marketplace had changed abruptly, and the demand for the industrial application of its technology had all but dried up overnight. But the company's technology remained sound, and employees had long been encouraged to scan the horizon for new and different applications. People at all levels were envisioning potential uses. One particularly promising idea surfaced: "What if our technology could do for the human body what it has done for industrial applications? Could it be used to rapidly and effectively clear blockages in arteries?" This question became the seed of a radical transformation. The company was able to shift gears much faster than most. They analyzed the possibilities, began exploring new product developments, and reached out to new markets. Pressure was intense to get up to speed as quickly as possible.

REDTECH was well on its way when I came to know them in the 1990s. Robert supervised 14 young and energetic managers in their late 20s and early 30s, all of whom were engineers. By nature, engineers are internally wired to look for problems and then fix them. This mind-set is a natural for focusing on what you don't want. But Robert was a firm believer in the power of vision and in focusing on what you *do* want. He also believed in management by walking around and engaging people. He was a tireless leader in helping others determine their passions, strengths, and values and, ultimately, helping them find positions and opportunities that were aligned with the company's mission, vision, and values.

Under Robert's guidance, REDTECH infused new procedures into its operations. Every interaction people had, from conversations to meetings to events, started the same way:

- This is our vision.
- What is your personal vision?
- Where are you right now with your personal vision and what you want?
- What do you as an individual, and we as a team, need to do to move things toward what you want?

Every employee in the division, from custodian to executive, was viewed as critical to its success and engaged in this process, articulating on a regular basis how they were contributing to the ultimate success of the organization. They each were encouraged to connect their personal job to the vision and values of the organization. Early on, if people said what they didn't want, Robert would urge them to instead clarify what they did want.

Robert recognized that change would not happen overnight. He walked around the manufacturing facility talking to people, telling stories, asking them questions to identify their wants, and then holding them accountable. And he never forgot! Robert would ask, "How many conversations will you have in the next week?" and then he would remember the number and follow up. He never forgot what he committed to, and he never forgot what they committed to. In the beginning, I think he probably annoyed some people, but his energy was hard to hate and the results impossible to dispute.

Two managers in particular, Tim and Brad, were enthusiastic supporters when Robert introduced the change in direction and began a series of 12-week training courses to help employees become self-guided, deal with the changes, and commit to lifelong learning. Each section of the program included a cross-section of the organization, with workers from the assembly line, finance, engineering, and regulatory affairs. The concept of aligning what people want personally and professionally and helping the organization focus on desired outcomes, even in light of significant change, really resonated with these young engineering managers. They were new to their tenures as leaders, but they had both experienced the ill effects of the unconscious focus on what we don't want to have happen. They immediately were proponents of the cause and became ambassadors (in the 20% group) who helped spread the philosophy to others.

Through every interaction and every opportunity, Robert, then his managers, and eventually other employees focused on their wants and helped each other self-correct and refocus when anyone veered off track. It became an integral part of the company's culture. Positive outcomes started happening. REDTECH's sales started increasing, issues with products were resolved, and improvements were made to production processes. Enthusiasm among the workforce grew along with the positive outcomes.

In a culture in which people are allowed and encouraged to play to their strengths, one of two scenarios will emerge, both of which benefit the organization in the long run:

1. Individuals recommit to the organization when they reconnect with their passions, strengths, and values and realize how well they are aligned with the company's vision and values. They clarify what they want, both personally and professionally, and create a plan of action to put their passions, strengths, and values to work. They once again see what originally drew them to the company. This was the case with Tim and Brad, the REDTECH managers who became even more enthusiastic supporters.

2. Individuals come to recognize that there is not a good fit with their current employer or work situation. That was the case with Carla, who was managed by Brad. No one had ever asked Carla what she really wanted. Once someone did, and she cautiously identified her true passions, interests, and strengths, the corporate culture Robert had created warmly embraced her discovery and encouraged her to pursue her true calling. She earned her degree and moved from the assembly line to the accounting department. In some environments, raising these questions would result in immediate problems. A positive-outcomes culture acknowledges that the realization of a fundamental disconnect will be the reality for some individuals. Allowing people to uncover and act on their true passions is far better for the individual and for the company, whether the employee stays or decides to go.

While the concept of playing to personal strengths has been around for decades, people still struggle with it. The Gallup organization estimates that a mere 20% of the workforce actually plays to its strengths regularly. My hope is that *Seeing Red Cars* provides tangible actions to help you take charge of your own destiny. There is great value in having individuals and teams engaged in a positive-outcomes mind-set and creating alignment within their organizations. The rapid rate of innovations in the marketplace presents challenges and opportunities in the same breath. In this environment, it is much easier for people to be critical and to slip into "I don't want" thoughts and fears. Instead, corporate America needs people who are *Seeing Red Cars* and able to turn on a dime in our environment of rapid change.

Not surprisingly, when we visited REDTECH 10 years later, many of the same people were there. It was like old home week. We scheduled interviews at three companies when we were filming *Seeing Red Cars,* and it was the third one we visited. Even though my project had ended about 10 years earlier, the employees we interviewed were a stark contrast. At the first two companies, when we asked employees what they want, they inevitably talked about what they didn't want. At REDTECH, the employees explained what their current challenges were and then clearly articulated what they wanted. We were stunned and impressed. The *Seeing Red Cars* culture was still alive and well and serving the company every day.

Leverage the Seeing Red Cars Culture

The environment in which we live is changing rapidly. Some organizations manage change well. Others make mistakes. Often, no one really knows what to do. As changes occur and the dust settles, people want to begin talking about it and playing a role in the movement toward better times. Employees who were asked to do things that do not sit well with them, such as taking on extra work following a downsizing or taking voluntary furloughs to ease payroll strain, want to talk about it and see their employers taking positive actions. Companies need to be courageous enough to have these conversations because if they don't, the grass may look greener elsewhere, and they could lose valuable people.

Companies are vying for the best and brightest talent while the hiring pool is shrinking. Every hour, 330 baby boomers (born 1946–1964) turn age 62, and there are 11% fewer Generation Xers (born 1965–1984) to fill their positions. That's about 36 fewer people every hour to backfill the holes left by retiring employees. Only 32% of companies have planned and strategized for the business implications of this reality. At the time this book was written, the economy was climbing out of a recession. We heard much about the shrinking workforce in the early 2000s. The economic downturn forced workforce reductions and caused older workers to remain in the workforce much longer. The recession has proven to be a distraction, simply delaying the inevitable. As the economy recovers, there will be a talent shortage. The people who are in control and driving with intention and high beams on will be in the best position to respond positively.

In turn, companies that are proactively *Seeing Red Cars* and driving with intention become magnets for the best and brightest talent. They will trump the demographic statistics and not be affected by the shrinking talent pool. These companies recognize that organizations are not big buildings pumping out products and services. Organizations are made up of *people* who want to do meaningful work, make a difference, and be acknowledged for their contributions.

The workforce is fluid, and marketplace demands are always changing. The makeup of the workforce can be different from day to day and from week to week because:

- Employees change roles rapidly.
- There are increasing numbers of independent contractors.
- Changing work environments call for changes in workers.

Smart executives understand that the messages they communicate today may be heard by a different set of ears than the ones they addressed last week. Therefore, they need to stay vigilant in their communication. Often the executives I work with grossly underestimate how many times they need to communicate the company's vision and values and tell the story in multiple ways: This is what we stand for, this is how we deliver on that promise, this is where we are going, and this is what is most important to us.

Organizations that clearly and regularly communicate their culture, values, and vision will thrive. They will attract the right folks at the right time and encourage their people to scan the marketplace, play to their passions and strengths, and define what they want, both personally and professionally. Alignment of company culture and attainment of corporate objectives will result. The greater the alignment, the greater the personal satisfaction, innovation, and solutions. Once your organization reaches critical mass with the *Seeing Red Cars* mind-set, it is easier to stay there. Less effort will be required to keep people engaged.

Companies that leverage their culture successfully replenish their stock by having the people who are serving them at any given time do so from a position of passion and strength. As people come and go, their companies' cultures are further strengthened by the successors' contributions. Companies that are *Seeing Red Cars* enjoy the following benefits:

- Employees and consumers bring their unique cultural experiences, which serve to strengthen the organization.

- Employees routinely scan the horizon and share their observations to enable the company to capitalize on new opportunities.

- Perceptions of the organization's culture are always accurate and strong because of its regular and consistent communication.

- Employees remain interested and engaged in the company's vision as it is regularly shared through powerful stories.

- The organization remains tightly integrated as everyone makes the best use of tools and technologies.

Through this keen awareness and open, consistent communication, organizations articulate a clear cultural identity and achieve high-quality talent management.

It All Begins with *You*

To close this book, we must come back from the team and organizational levels to focus on the individual. It is easy to look out our windows and criticize neighbors who are messy or creating some kind of nuisance. In the workplace, it is equally easy to look at the helm of dysfunctional units and find faults. In reality, in either situation, you can take action from where you are. We each play a critical role in building successful corporate cultures by taking personal responsibility and acting on what we *can* control. It is what we must do if we are serious about making positive things happen.

If we focus on what we can control in our own particular areas, then in our groups, then collectively as groups, imagine the difference it could make. A song by talented songwriter Jordyn Shellhart, whom I interviewed for *Life to the Max,* exemplifies this truth from the perspective of our homes and neighborhoods. What makes this story even more amazing is the mature insight she expresses at such a tender age. Jordyn was only 15 years old when she wrote this song.

Save the Neighborhood

I had a dream that I could make this whole world different
Don't ask me why
I can't say, it's just a feeling
With all my overthinking I've been thinking way too big
'cause if I try to keep it simple there's so much more
    I can give

I've made up my mind
It's the only thing that won't be changing
No more wasting time
I mean just what I'm saying
I've made my resolutions but they've always come and gone
In the mirror I can see a revolution coming on

You gotta crawl before you walk
You gotta walk before you run
Gotta get through the raging storms
Before you can taste the morning sun
So I'm stepping right outside my door
And spreading my light that shines so good
Cause if you want to save the world
You gotta save the neighborhood

Instead of throwing stones at the powers that be, you have the
capacity to impact your own job, work area, peers, and projects.
Let's all take responsibility to focus on what we can control and
on what impact we can have.

Thank you for driving with intention and learning how to
implement *Seeing Red Cars* in your own life.

Now, go out and make a difference in the world.

Laura Goodrich

This book is dedicated to Joel Suzucki *(2/11/1948–8/8/2009), who
was the inspiration for Seeing Red Cars.*

Seeing Red Cars Visual, Auditory, and Tactile "Triggers"

U se a combination of these methods to act as "triggers" to jog your memory and retain your focus on what you want.

Visual Triggers

- Post-it Notes strategically placed around your home and office.
- Automatic e-mail sent to yourself each week (e.g., list of "I want" statements).
- *Seeing Red Cars* Cards in your wallet, pocket, or purse (www. seeingredcarsbook.com).
- *Seeing Red Cars* Visualization on the calendar daily.
- *Seeing Red Cars* "I Want" Statements app for cell phone (see http://seeingredcarsbook.com).
- *Seeing Red Cars* Video app available on iTunes (see http:// seeingredcarsbook.com).
- Review *Seeing Red Cars* Toolkit weekly.
- *Seeing Red Cars* screensaver (see http://seeingredcarsbook. com).

- Paint red a door, a chair, or another object you see daily in your home or office.

Auditory Triggers

- *Seeing Red Cars* Friends committed to your success, ready to remind you of your commitment to focus on what you want, on the *Seeing Red Cars* opportunities.

- *Seeing Red Cars* Audio Stories available on iTunes: Listen to a story weekly. (see http://seeingredcarsbook.com).

- Listen to a song with lyrics that remind you of what you want.

Tactile Triggers

- Print *Seeing Red Cars* business-card-size reminder cards to write in your top "I want" statements and carry them with you (www.seeingredcarsbook.com).

- Wear red clothing or accessories as reminders to think about what you want.

- Buy a red car ;)

- Buy *Seeing Red Cars* accessories to create visual and tactile reminders of what you want (see http://seeingredcarsbook. com).

Seeing Red Cars
Toolkit At-a-Glance

Tool 1

Tool 2 (same as Tool 7)

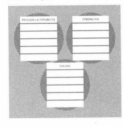

Tool 3

Tool 4

Tool 5

Tool 6

Tool 7 (same as Tool 2)

Tool 8

Tool 9

Tool 10

Tool 11

Tool 12

Acknowledgments

*T*his book was born out of a 40-year-plus journey of wanting to have a powerfully positive impact, my unquenchable desire to understand what it takes to accomplish what we want personally and professionally, and a deep passion to help teams and organizations create positive change through the power of their people. I have sought to create a shift from the unconscious focus on what we are trying to avoid and what we fear to an intentional focus on what we want individually and collectively.

GREG STIEVER, my business partner, saw and recognized the value of that vision and helped me frame it for the concept of the film *Seeing Red Cars*. Thank you, Greg, for first recognizing the spark and for being a brave leader and a legendary director-producer, filmmaker, storyteller, and truly one of the best entrepreneurs and friends I could ever ask for. Here's to a long and successful journey. I am proud to be your business partner.

In 2006, Greg and I introduced our first business film concept (now *Seeing Red Cars*) to JOEL SUZUCKI of Star Thrower Distribution, an international distributor of training and development videos and multimedia productions. Joel believed in the film from the beginning and inspired the name *Seeing Red Cars* and every aspect of the film from start to finish! Sadly, Joel lost his battle with cancer in August 2009. This book is dedicated to him. Despite

Joel's passing, his sage wisdom and kindness guided me through every aspect of writing this book. I will always remember Joel and feel grateful for the faith he placed in me, Greg Stiever, and our organization, On Impact. The film *Seeing Red Cars* has started the wheels rolling in the right direction by creating awareness and inviting people to focus on what they want rather than on what they are trying to avoid. Thank you to Melanie Gray for her excellent writing and insight and to Todd Adams and all our friends at Star Thrower for representing the film so expertly! The film and concept behind *Seeing Red Cars* would never have gained the audience it has without you. While grateful for the success of the film, I felt the need to dig deeper and truly help people, teams, and organizations create lasting change through focus and actions toward positive outcomes, toward a *Seeing Red Cars* mind-set. That's what this book offers.

I am deeply grateful that David Marshall of Berrett-Koehler Publishing saw the *Seeing Red Cars* film and urged Johanna Vondeling at Berrett-Koehler to explore our vision for a *Seeing Red Cars* book. It is hard to put into words the gratitude I feel for people like David and Johanna who see the possibilities of a concept and help make it even bigger and more powerful. Johanna has played this role in my life and the vision of *Seeing Red Cars*. Her keen sense of the big picture, coupled with a laser eye for the minute details, made a world of difference. I am also grateful to be a part of the Berrett-Koehler mission of creating a world that works for all, and I greatly appreciate the expertise and commitment of Neal Maillet, Jeevan Sivasubramaniam, Kristen Frantz, Katie Sheehan, Michael Crowley, Bonnie Kaufman, Richard Wilson, Dianne Platner, and their respective teams. Berrett-Koehler is an organization that operates with a *Seeing Red Cars* mind-set at its best!

Throughout my life I have been blessed to have so many people who have supported me both personally and professionally. The wisdom and backing I have received from them are the heart of this book, and the many courageous stories of passionate leaders I have worked with are the soul.

I am deeply grateful to the amazing people who have enhanced my life and my life's work through our thousands of conversations, sessions, and interactions. This book is a culmination of all that I have learned from you. Thank you:

Carol Anderson	Kris Peterson
Tim Anderson	Martha Pomerantz
Leo Bottary	Cali Ressler
David Chard	Brad Roberts
Tom DeBolt	Kristy Roberts
Jim Dittmer	Russell Schoneberger
Adam Dustus	Tom Schultz
Michelle Florin	Anne Sharockman
Tim Fuller	Mark Sharockman
Lesa Hammond	Jordyn Shellhart
Jeff Hurinenko	Kim Smith
Gary Judd	Mark Spanjers
Roz Keppler	Mark Stenion
Roger Kuehn	Nick Tasler
Peter Leyden	Jodi Thompson
Billy McLaughlin	Dr. Ellen Weber
Carla Ness Luedtke	Tom Wojick
Amy Olsen-Zastrow	Cliff Young
Dr. Nancy Perkins	Lisa Zigarmi
Dr. Anne Perschell	

Thank you to WENDY MEADLEY and LAURI FLAQUER, who have helped shape our marketing efforts with *Seeing Red Cars* and On Impact. Thank you to DAYNA HANENBURG, my dear and longtime friend and graphic artist for creating the *Seeing Red Cars* Toolkit and JEAN KINDEM for making it such an accessible and powerful tool. And many thanks to our talented scriptwriter, LILY

Coyle, for writing the script for the *Seeing Red Cars* film, and Bekki Freeman, who developed the *Seeing Red Cars* apps.

I believe that most authors would be well served to have an amazing copyeditor or writer by their side—someone above and beyond the publisher's editors who can pull it all together and separate the wheat from the chaff, as they say. In my case, this was a necessity! I know my strengths, and I know my weaknesses. Copywriting is not my strength, but it is the extraordinary strength of my powerhouse business writer, Diane Autey. She took my disjointed, transcribed audio segments and composed well-organized, conversational chapters. Without her expertise, honesty, and seasoned skill, this book would never have been written!

As you will see in this book, I discuss the importance of three different types of supporters in our lives. I have been blessed with so many. Again, to all of you, my heartfelt thanks.

Thank you to my "Been There Done That" supporters: Don Tapscott, Billy McLaughlin, and Robert Scott.

Thank you to my "Walk a Mile in Another's Shoes" friend and colleague on a similar journey: Lisa Jansa, CEO of Exsulin Corporation.

And thank you to my "I'll Always Love You but That Doesn't Mean I Won't Challenge Your Assumptions" supporters. They are the bright, shining stars I feel privileged to share my life with: Leah Jensen, Marcia Dolphin, and my sister Sybil Judd.

To my children, Madi and Judd, who inspire me every day, I am so proud of the amazing young adults you have become. Never stop focusing on what you want! The world will be a better place because of it.

And last but most certainly not least, to my husband, Rick Goodrich, who has supported me every step of the way and is a clear example of focusing on and getting what you want. I am truly blessed to have you as my husband.

Notes

Introduction

"Law of Attraction" Jack Canfield and D. D. Watkins, *Jack Canfield's Key to Living the Law of Attraction: A Simple Guide to Creating the Life of Your Dreams* (Deerfield Beach, FL: Health Communications, 2007), pp. 1–10.

"Malcolm Gladwell's book *Outliers*" Malcolm Gladwell, *Outliers: The Story of Success* (New York: Little, Brown, 2008), p. 21.

Chapter 1

"50,000 thoughts" Price Pritchett, *Hard Optimism: How to Succeed in a World Where Positive Wins* (New York: McGraw-Hill, 2007), p. 82.

"20% are very open and excited" Price Pritchett interview on Charlie Greer blog: How to deal with change – An interview with Dr. Price Pritchett.

"MITA Brain Institute" Ellen Weber, Blog: "Expect Neuron Pathways to Dynamic Solutions," at www.brainleadersandlearners.com/serotonin/expect-neuron-pathways-to-solutions/; MITA Brain Institute (2009), at http://www.mitaleadership.com.

"two common beliefs get in the way" Peter M. Senge, *The Fifth Discipline: The Art & Practice of the Learning Organization* (New York: Doubleday, 1990), p. 145.

"The Fifth Discipline" Peter M. Senge, *The Fifth Discipline: The Art & Practice of the Learning Organization* (New York: Doubleday, 1990), p. 155.

"fear and concern" Ellen Weber, Blog: "Expect Neuron Pathways to Dynamic Solutions."

"50,000 thoughts" Price Pritchett, *Hard Optimism*, p. 82.

"Standing in the Fire" Larry Dressler, *Standing in the Fire: Leading High-Heat Meetings with Clarity, Calm, and Courage* (San Francisco: Berrett-Koehler, 2010), pp. 80–86.

"mirror neurons" PBS, *Nova Science Now*, "Mirror Neurons" (2005), at www.pbs. org/wgbh/nova/sciencenow/3204/01.html.

"Army War College" Bob Johansen, *Leaders Make the Future: Ten New Leadership Skills for an Uncertain World* (San Francisco: Berrett-Koehler, 2009), pp. 1–14.

"20% are very open and excited" Price Pritchett interview on Charlie Greer blog: How to deal with change—An interview with Dr. Price Pritchett.

"the five C's" Price Pritchett interview on Charlie Greer blog: How to deal with change—An interview with Dr. Price Pritchett.

Chapter 3

"StrengthsFinder 2.0" Tom Rath, *StrengthsFinder 2.0* (New York: Gallup Press, 2007), pp. 11–13.

"Now, Discover Your Strengths" Marcus Buckingham and Donald O.Clifton, *Now, Discover Your Strengths* (New York: The Free Press, 2001), p. 6.

"the Deluxe Corporation" Nick Tasler, Conversation, 2010 Deluxe Knowledge Exchange; see www.deluxeknowledgexchange.com.

Chapter 4

"Don Tapscott" Don Tapscott, coauthor of *Wikinomics* and *Macrowikinomics*, Speech, Minneapolis, 2010.

"On The Edge of the Digital Age" Peter Leyden, *On the Edge of the Digital Age*, four-part newspaper series, 1994, at http://ww2.startribune.com/stonline/html/digage/logfx.htm.

"Jeffrey Hurinenko" Jeffrey Hurinenko, TV: "Art Is a Journey," on *Life to the Max* (www.lifetothemax.tv/; for Life Touch, see www.lifetouch.com/); for Jeffrey Hurinenko's work, see www.jeffreyhurinenko.com/.

"a mere 20% of the workforce" Marcus Buckingham and Donald O. Clifton, *Gallup Management Journal*, "The Strengths Revolution," at http://gmj.gallup. com/content/547/the-strengths-revolution.aspxreplace.

"Futurist Jim Carroll" Jim Carroll, Blog, "10 Things That Are True about the Future," at www.jimcarroll.com/blog/2010/03/10-things-that-are-true-about. html.

"Anne Pershel" Ann Pershel, *Germane Consulting* blog, "Good Leaders See into the Future," at http://germaneconsulting.com/good-leaders-see-into-the-future/.

"Results-Only Work Environment (ROWE)" Cali Ressler and Jody Thompson, *Why Work Sucks and How to Fix It* (New York: Portfolio, 2008), pp. 11–16.

Chapter 5

"Author Daniel Pink" Daniel H. Pink, *Drive: The Surprising Truth about What Motivates Us* (New York: Riverhead, 2009), p. 47.

"Peter Senge's tension illustration" Peter M. Senge, *The Fifth Discipline*, pp. 142–150.

"the Pareto principle" Richard Koch, *The 80/20 Principle: The Secret to Achieving More with Less* (New York: Crown Business, 1999), p. 6.

Chapter 6

"an estimated 70% of their thoughts" Price Pritchett, *Hard Optimism*, p. 78.

"In Daniel Pink's book Drive" Daniel H. Pink, *Drive*, p. 47.

Chapter 7

"Nick Tasler" Nick Tasler, "Prime Your Mind for Action," *Business Week*, citing Shelley Taylor and Peter Gollwitzer, at www.businessweek.com/managing/content/nov2009/ca2009113_110290.htm.

"The Brain That Changes Itself" Norman Doidge, *The Brain That Changes Itself: Stories of Personal Triumph from the Frontiers of Brain Science* (New York: Penguin, 2007).

"In *First Things First*" Stephen Covey, A. Roger Merrill, and Rebecca R. Merrill, *First Things First* (New York: Simon & Schuster, 1994), pp. 32–43.

"The Little School System That Could" Daniel L. Duke, *The Little School System That Could: Transforming a City School District* (Albany: State University of New York Press, 2008), pp. 1–8.

Chapter 8

"famous cathedral story" Sister Joan Chittister, *The Rule of Benedict: Insights for the Ages* (New York: Crossroad, 2002).

"a mere 20% of the workforce" Marcus Buckingham and Donald O. Clifton, *Gallup Management Journal*, "The Strengths Revolution," at http://gmj.gallup.com/content/547/the-strengths-revolution.aspxreplace.

"Only 32% of companies" According to Sarah Sladek, President and CEO, Limelight Generations, Interview on Generations, 2010.

Conclusion

"songwriter Jordyn Shellhart" Jordyn Shellhart, Vocals, Lyrics: Rick Barker, Britton Cameron, Jordyn Shellhart Song: "Save the Neighborhood" (2009).

Additional Resources

Ed Oakley and Doug Krug, *Enlightened Leadership: Getting to the Heart of Change* (New York: Fireside, 1991), Chapter 5, "Looking at Focus."

Nancy Perkins (1931–2003), Course: Accent on Learning!

Vickie Halsey, PhD, specializes in creating brain-based and accelerated learning strategies, Kenneth Blanchard Companies, at http://www.kenblanchard.com/About_Ken_Blanchard_Companies/Keynote_Speakers/Victoria_Halsey/.

Pam Richardson, *The Life Coach: Become the Person You've always Wanted To Be* (London: Hamlyn, 2004).

Dawn Brewer, Wheel of Life coaching tool from http://personaldevelopment.suite101.com/article.cfm/what_is_a_wheel_of_life.

Marsha Freedman, "Visualize Your Success! Power Up Your Mind for Positive Outcome," from http://www.internetviz-newsletters.com/PSJ/e_article001084685.cfm?x=b11.0.

Gina Trapani, "How to Mitigate Urgent to Focus on the Important," *Harvard Business Review*, February 2009, at http://blogs.hbr.org/cs/2009/02/how_to_mitigate_the_urgent_to.html.

Index

About the Author

*F*or the last 25 years, Laura Goodrich has honed her international expertise in workplace dynamics as a speaker, corporate trainer, coach, film producer, and author. She has coached and advised hundreds of executives, business leaders, teams, and organizations through periods of change and transition, in even the most challenging workplace environments. She is recognized as an expert in workplace dynamics, change, and the future of work.

The catalyst for the popular *Seeing Red Cars* film, and now the book that delves deeper into the philosophy and practice of focusing on what you want, is her experiences: "Time and time again, I have witnessed the cascading effect of the natural tendency to focus on what we don't want, especially in workplaces dealing with a corporate change. The rare view that I had allowed me to see the avalanche quality of this focus on what we don't want and can't control. I realized that with awareness and effort, this whole mindset can be pointed, instead, toward positive outcomes. That natural negative tendency will dominate until people and organizations make a conscious decision to focus intentionally on what they do want. It begins one person at a time and then grows. Once a critical mass has made this change, and the *Seeing Red Cars* mind-set becomes a part of the organization's modus operandi, it becomes an automatic and anticipated way of running meetings, setting objectives, discussing projects, and finding solutions."

Laura has worked with a wide range of industries, including consulting, biomedical, medical, education, manufacturing, high tech, and retail, and with companies such as Deloitte, Wells Fargo, Medtronic, Medrad Possis, and American Express. Her degree is in Training and Organizational Development from the University of Minnesota. She is a member of the American Society for Training and Development (ASTD) and the National Speakers Association (NSA) and has received coach training from both the Corporate Coach University and the Coaches Training Institute.

Laura is cofounder of On Impact, an integrated content company that specializes in creating and producing videos, television, and multimedia content delivered over time to create sustained change and adoption of important leadership concepts. Its first film, *Seeing Red Cars,* is distributed by Star Thrower, internationally the second largest distributor of leadership videos. The film is used in training sessions or to kick off or close important meetings.

On Impact develops videos and a comprehensive process to support organizational initiatives and change called Driving It Home. The company's vision is to produce at least 10 videos similar to *Seeing Red Cars*, companion books to the videos, and complementary promotional products.

Laura typically makes presentations 30 to 50 times a year and often engages in longer-term projects multiple times over the course of a year or more. On Impact is committed to creating lasting change, and she feels strongly about spacing learning over time. For this reason, On Impact has created a concept called "Extend the Experience." Users either watch or read online a two- to three-minute "refresher segment" on their own initiative. It is highlighted here: www.onimpactproductions.com/extend-the-experience/.

On Impact will be publishing a newsletter to highlight how people are using the film, the book, and the *Seeing Red Cars* promotional products. We want you to be a part of the process and encourage you to keep sharing your amazing stories! Go to www.seeingredcarsbook.com for the details. Additionally, we develop what we call "hero stories," where we tell the story of a customer who is using *Seeing Red Cars*. Hero stories are available on our Web site, tweeted via Twitter, and broadcast to clients from Star Thrower. These stories highlight our customers' creativity and generate additional training ideas for other customers. They can be accessed here: www.onimpactproductions.com/seeing-red-car-hero-stories/.

Laura lives in Lakeville, Minnesota, with her husband, daughter, and son. You can visit the book's Web site at www.seeingredcarsbook.com.

Berrett–Koehler
BK Publishers

Berrett-Koehler is an independent publisher dedicated to an ambitious mission: *Creating a World That Works for All*.

We believe that to truly create a better world, action is needed at all levels—individual, organizational, and societal. At the individual level, our publications help people align their lives with their values and with their aspirations for a better world. At the organizational level, our publications promote progressive leadership and management practices, socially responsible approaches to business, and humane and effective organizations. At the societal level, our publications advance social and economic justice, shared prosperity, sustainability, and new solutions to national and global issues.

A major theme of our publications is "Opening Up New Space." Berrett-Koehler titles challenge conventional thinking, introduce new ideas, and foster positive change. Their common quest is changing the underlying beliefs, mindsets, institutions, and structures that keep generating the same cycles of problems, no matter who our leaders are or what improvement programs we adopt.

We strive to practice what we preach—to operate our publishing company in line with the ideas in our books. At the core of our approach is stewardship, which we define as a deep sense of responsibility to administer the company for the benefit of all of our "stakeholder" groups: authors, customers, employees, investors, service providers, and the communities and environment around us.

We are grateful to the thousands of readers, authors, and other friends of the company who consider themselves to be part of the "BK Community." We hope that you, too, will join us in our mission.

A BK Life Book

This book is part of our BK Life series. BK Life books change people's lives. They help individuals improve their lives in ways that are beneficial for the families, organizations, communities, nations, and world in which they live and work. To find out more, visit **www.bk-life.com**.

Berrett–Koehler
Publishers

A community dedicated to creating
a world that works for all

Visit Our Website: www.bkconnection.com

Read book excerpts, see author videos and Internet movies, read
our authors' blogs, join discussion groups, download book apps, find
out about the BK Affiliate Network, browse subject-area libraries of
books, get special discounts, and more!

Subscribe to Our Free E-Newsletter, the *BK Communiqué*

Be the first to hear about new publications, special discount offers,
exclusive articles, news about bestsellers, and more! Get on the list
for our free e-newsletter by going to **www.bkconnection.com**.

Get Quantity Discounts

Berrett-Koehler books are available at quantity discounts for orders
of ten or more copies. Please call us toll-free at (800) 929-2929 or
email us at bkp.orders@aidcvt.com.

Join the BK Community

BKcommunity.com is a virtual meeting place where people from
around the world can engage with kindred spirits to create a world
that works for all. BKcommunity.com members may create their own
profiles, blog, start and participate in forums and discussion groups,
post photos and videos, answer surveys, announce and register for
upcoming events, and chat with others online in real time. Please join
the conversation!